"*Behind and Beyond the Badge* is a fast and most interesting read, especially for someone not directly in the field of law enforcement but works with college students of various ages and backgrounds who aspire to become sworn law enforcement officers. It really struck home with me. Donna Brown presents men and women who have committed themselves to careers 'in the trenches' as first responders and clearly shows some of the good, the bad and the ugly of the profession and the important work they do every day. It is an important book, and I hope to have each of my seniors read it as they graduate and embark upon their careers in law enforcement. *Behind and Beyond the Badge* has a strong message and should be required reading in every Criminal Justice program."

DAVID PERSKY, PH.D., J.D.
Professor of Criminal Justice
Saint Leo University

"Retired Homicide Sergeant Donna Brown is a master storyteller. Her book is a captivating read about first responders who share their personal thoughts about working in high-stress positions. If you want to really understand what it's like to do their jobs, know someone who is thinking about a career as a first responder, or a family member of a first responder, then this book is a must-read."

FLOY TURNER
FDLE Special Agent (Retired)
Best-Selling Author

"In Volume II of her award-winning BEHIND AND BEYOND THE BADGE series, Donna Brown once again takes us behind the scenes into the lives of first responders and their families. The no-nonsense approach of her writing lets the individuals' stories speak for themselves, and they leave indelible impressions on the reader's mind. Brown's book covers a wide range of experiences: the day-to-day operations of a sheriff's department aviation unit, the intensity of dispatch operations, gut-wrenching experiences in highway patrol, and a mother's grief at the loss of her police sergeant son are just a few of the stories she includes. This book should be required reading for law enforcement academies and criminology departments, and I recommend it to anyone who wants to understand what the 'thin blue line' really means."

A. E. HOWE
Author of the Amazon Best-selling *Larry Macklin Mysteries* Series

Behind and Beyond the Badge

Volume II

MORE STORIES FROM THE VILLAGE OF FIRST RESPONDERS WITH COPS, FIREFIGHTERS, EMS, DISPATCHERS, FORENSICS, AND VICTIM ADVOCATES

DONNA BROWN

Storehouse Media Group, LLC
Jacksonville, FL

BEHIND AND BEYOND THE BADGE Volume II: More Stories from the Village of First Responders with Cops, Firefighters, EMS, Dispatchers, Forensics, and Victim Advocates

Copyright © 2018 by Donna Brown

All rights reserved. No part of this publication may be reproduced, distributed, or transmitted in any form or by any means, including photocopying, recording, or other electronic or mechanical methods, without the prior written permission of the author, except in the case of brief quotations embodied in critical reviews and certain other noncommercial uses permitted by copyright law. For permission requests, email author at email address below and type in subject line: "Attention: Permissions Coordinator."

Donna Brown

Tallahassee, Florida 32317
www.BehindAndBeyondTheBadge.com
Donna@DonnaBrownAuthor.com

Ordering Information:

Quantity sales. Special discounts are available with the author at the email address above and type in subject line "Special Sales Department."

Publisher Information:

Storehouse Media Group, LLC
Jacksonville, Florida 32256
Hello@StorehouseMediaGroup.com

The views expressed in this work are solely those of the author and do not necessarily reflect the views of the publisher, and the publisher hereby disclaims any responsibility for them.

Cover design by Katie Campbell
Author Photo by Red Fly Studios

Behind and Beyond the Badge Volume II / Donna Brown —1st ed.

ISBN-13: 978-1-943106-40-0 (hardcover)
ISBN-13: 978-1-943106-41-7 (paperback)
ISBN-13: 978-1-943106-42-4 (ebook)

Library of Congress Control Number: 2017940797

Printed in the United States of America

Dedication

To those who did the job.
To those who do the job.
To all first responders who have lost their lives doing the job.
To the families left behind.

"We will remember every rescuer who died in honor.
We will remember every family that lives in grief.
We will remember…"

-- George W. Bush --

43rd President of the United States of America

Contents

Introduction 1

Law Enforcement Officers 5

   1: Sergeant Donna Brown 7

   2: Sergeant Scott Angulo 21

   3: Officer Deborah Powell 39

   4: Lieutenant James Fairfield 47

   5: Corporal Trish England 61

   6: K9 Sergeant David Bell 69

   7: Chief Bob Stewart 80

   8: Commander Susan Jeter 93

   9: Andrew McClenahan 100

   10: Special Agent Alan Lopez 119

   11: Lieutenant Lee Majors 135

   12: Sergeant Tina Haddon 149

   13: Captain Rory Robbins 163

   14: Special Agent Supervisor Tonja Bryant-Smith 175

The Village Of First Responders 183

   15: Betty Green 185

   16: Deputy Chief Mac Kemp 192

   17: Division Chief Andrea Jones 205

   18: Public Safety Communications Operator William Blanton ... 215

   19: Deputy Director Andy Parker 224

   20: Victim Advocate Melanie Tudor 232

About the Author DONNA BROWN 245

Introduction

I wrote the first *Behind and Beyond the Badge* for a variety of reasons, but there was one underlying thought that was my primary motivator. Police officers and the law enforcement profession as a whole were on the receiving end of predominantly negative media attention. As a twenty-six-year veteran police officer, it hurt and made me sad because I know that overwhelmingly, cops are good people. Most folks see just a badge. Behind and beyond the badge is what people need to know, the person, a person who is no different than they are. They just put on a different uniform to go to work.

Volume I afforded me some amazing opportunities. My favorite has been speaking engagements. I've spoken to university criminal justice students and faculty, to civic groups, professional organizations, book clubs, and at book stores. No group or venue has been too large or too small; they're all opportunities to have open and honest conversations about cops, the law enforcement profession, and all first responders. The dialogue has been eye-opening for me and for the audiences.

With most of those in attendance, two things usually come up. The media and the perception versus reality and the fact that most people really don't understand. They don't know what officers and other first responders really do or the toll it takes physically and emotionally. The wonderful thing is that they truly seem to want to know more. Specific tasks, training, work hours/shifts, investigations, forensics......their questions have covered so many topics.

I always ask if they know what happens or could happen when they call for help. The simple and correct answer is that they call and someone comes. But I give them this scenario.

First, someone has to answer their phone call and gather critical information. That information is passed onto a dispatcher, who then sends the appropriate unit. For the sake of discussion, I tell them to imagine it is a police officer.

Once that officer arrives, they have to assess the situation quickly. They may notify the dispatcher that they need backup, the fire department, Emergency Medical Services, forensics, a detective, and/or a victim advocate. They've made one call for help, and it can result in any or all of those people coming to their aid. As I describe this scenario, I literally see eyes widen and jaws drop. People truly have no idea how this works.

Most people understand that police officers, firefighters, and Emergency Medical Services are first responders but give little thought to others who may not be directly on the front lines but are a crucial part of the process. For fifteen years, I was in charge of various investigative units in our department's Criminal Investigation Division. Ten of those years I supervised the Homicide Unit and the Victim Advocate Unit. I could have never done my job without all of these other people, and they get very little recognition or credit. They are all what I call the Village of First Responders.

Dispatchers are every first responder's life line; they're that calming voice in the dark. They have mastered the art of multi-tasking and save lives. They talk small children through traumatic situations while trying to determine where they are so that they can send help to their injured or sick parent. They talk people through childbirth, choking incidents, and basic first aid, all while trying to keep these folks calm until a first responder arrives. They do all of this without the luxury of sight. While they don't fear for their personal safety, they do for those on the other end of the radio. They work long shifts, shiftwork, nights, weekends, and holidays. It's a stressful profession. I could not imagine my books without them being represented.

Television and films have brought the forensic profession to the forefront. But often they are depicted in clean, sterile environments. People know that they respond to crime scenes but really don't understand what they do or the training it requires. They don't think about what they see. In order to process a crime scene, they have to get into it. Blood, decaying bodies, body parts, autopsies, they see the results of the worse things that one human being can do to another. They have to set that aside and do their job and do it well. In many departments, they're on call, work nights, weekends, and holidays. It's not a job for everyone. My books would not be complete without their representation.

I came from a department that fortunately had a full-time, fully staffed Victim Advocate Unit. They too respond to active crime scenes. They help people who have experienced terrible loss or a traumatic event and often work with them through the criminal justice system process. Many remain in contact with their victims for years. Our victim advocates were on call and worked nights, weekends, and holidays too. Does anyone ever call a victim advocate when they're having a good day? No, they too deal with the dark side of reality. I feel for departments that don't have such a unit, but for me, they will always be a part of the Village of First Responders.

In my first book, I included a woman whose husband was killed in the line of duty. For this book, I have included a mother whose son was killed in the line of duty, one of my coworkers. The public often sees the initial news when an officer is killed and maybe a little about the funeral, but then life goes on. For these families left behind, life goes on too, but the hurt and pain is always with them, just like anyone else who has lost a cherished family member. I had to include them in my books.

Because of the discussions with various groups, I've taken this book and the stories a little deeper. The folks in the first book opened their hearts and shared some amazing thoughts. I've asked the people in this book to do the same in describing career-defining moments, the training it takes to do their jobs, the best part of their jobs and the most difficult. They also bared their souls, and their words are at times gut-wrenchingly honest. I can't thank them enough for their willingness to be a part of this book and to help get my intended message out there. First responders are first and foremost human.

Volume I of *Behind and Beyond the Badge* won two gold medals in nonfiction categories in the Florida Authors and Publishers President's Book Awards, a national competition. It was a sign for me that the word is getting out.

My books may not have the power to change minds, but by offering a different perspective, perhaps I can open them!

LAW ENFORCEMENT OFFICERS

Sergeant Donna Brown

Tallahassee Police Department
Retired: Twenty-Six Years of Service

When I wrote Volume One of ***Behind and Beyond the Badge***, I had no intention of including my story in the book. Those who know best about writing a book encouraged me to write something about myself. Injecting my story would provide credibility because I know its topic well.

As I have told those included within these pages, writing about yourself is difficult, and it is for me as well. But the feedback that I received from Volume One has been amazing with a consistent theme. People don't know what goes on behind and beyond the badge, but they truly want to know more – more detail and more personal thoughts from those who do and have done the job.

For this reason, I've asked those in this book to dig a little deeper in talking about the job they do or did do. I thought it only fair that I do the same.

I graduated from Florida State University (FSU) in August 1979 with a bachelor of science degree in criminology. In truth, I had no desire to become a police officer; I wanted to just springboard straight to investigator and work with kids, but every job to which I applied rejected me. They only wanted applicants who had three to five years of law enforcement experience.

One day, I was just about tapped out of money. Then I saw an ad in the local newspaper—the Tallahassee Police Department (TPD) was hiring. I applied. The hiring process wasn't what it is today, but it included a background investigation, a polygraph, a physical examination, an interview, and physical agility tests. I had to run, lift, carry, and pull exactly what the male applicants had to do. It wasn't easy, but I passed.

That October, TPD hired me, and I went on to attend the police academy.

At that time, I was one of only five women at our department of nearly one hundred fifty officers. (Our department now has over 400 sworn officers.) Upon completion of the academy, I returned to TPD and began my training. Female police officers were still a new concept to the department and to the city of Tallahassee as a whole, which provided for interesting times and challenges.

I was assigned to a squad with a mixture of young officers and those with more experience. My sergeant had been on the job for many years, as had my shift lieutenant.

The first training officer I was assigned was younger, and I was the first new officer he had been tasked with training. While I learned from him, it was a rocky road. My sergeant and some of the other officers recognized this, and I was eventually switched to a veteran officer. He was a "no-nonsense" guy but believed in doing the right thing, all the time, and treated everyone with respect. Those things, along with his work ethic, set the tone for my career.

Nothing but a Bloody Nose

I completed my training and attained solo status, meaning that I was assigned to a patrol zone and began answering calls for service on my own. While working one day, I was sent as a backup officer to a domestic call. Probable cause was established to take the husband into custody, but he was not keen on going to jail. A physical altercation ensued, and eventually he was handcuffed and taken into custody.

When it was over, the primary officer told me my nose was bleeding. I didn't even realize it. Our sergeant arrived on scene and asked if I was okay. I told him yes, completed our paperwork for the arrest, and finished my shift.

When I came to work the next day, my sergeant again asked if I was okay. My answer was the same: yes. He recapped my last twenty-four hours: I had endured a bloody nose, didn't cry, didn't go home, and I came back to work the next day ready for my shift. Apparently, I had passed the "test," and I had been accepted.

Community Acceptance

While finally being accepted by my peers, it took the community a bit longer. I was dispatched to a bar fight at one of our finer local establishments. One individual was still on the scene; the other had left.

When I arrived, I was met by a gentleman whose face had been rather bloodied. While he told me what had transpired, a second officer arrived. When he saw the other officer, a male, he told me, "Oh good, a real police officer is here," and immediately went to him and began telling his story. This officer told the gentleman that he needed to go back and talk to me as I was the primary officer and would be assisting him.

He continued to argue that he only wanted to talk to the "real" police officer. I said nothing. The other officer looked at me and said we both needed to leave; apparently this gentleman didn't need our assistance. Again, I said nothing, but we both walked to our respective police cars.

The gentleman began asking where we were going, stating that we couldn't leave without helping him. The other officer told him that either he would speak to me, or we were, in fact, leaving. He kept looking at both of us and finally agreed to talk with me.

I've often looked back at those early times and truly believe they helped shape me, not only as a police officer, but as a person. I was judged on my gender and size, not on my knowledge or skill. I vowed that I would never approach or treat someone in that manner, at work or in my personal life. While not perfect, I feel that philosophy served me well, and still does.

I ask everyone in the book to tell me about what they consider to be a career-defining moment for them. For some it has been obvious and easy to talk about; for others, just the opposite. In my first book, I personally talked about two situations that stood out to me. I purposefully left the following scenario out. I've mentioned it to a few people over the years but have never really talked about the enormous impact it had on me. It, too, helped shape the rest of my career.

A Close Call

It was a normal day at work. A call went out over the radio that an armed robbery had just occurred at a business. I wasn't far from the location and advised dispatch that I would respond.

They provided a description of the suspect and his clothing and that he had a firearm.

Instead of taking some of the main roads to the business, I decided to take an alternate route through a nearby neighborhood. A person matching the description came running around a corner and almost hit my patrol car. I stopped, advised dispatch of my location and that I was now in foot pursuit.

Imagine running as fast as you can, wearing thirty pounds of gear, and trying to talk on the police radio letting dispatch and other officers know where you are and what direction you're heading. I caught up to the suspect. He had boxed himself in with nowhere to go.

Knowing he was allegedly armed, I focused on him and his hands. His back was to me, but his arms were in front of him. I couldn't see his hands. I had drawn my service weapon and began giving him verbal commands, telling him to raise his hands and get on the ground. I told dispatch that I had the suspect cornered at gunpoint. When they asked me exactly where I was, I couldn't tell them. A huge mistake.

The suspect slowly turned to face me, a gun in his right hand by his side. He kept looking around as if trying to find a way to escape. There was no place for me to take cover; we were facing each other about thirty feet apart. Another mistake.

He continued to ignore my commands. I was yelling at him to drop the gun. I could feel my finger on the trigger; I was slowly beginning to pull it back. My heart was pounding. I was still yelling at him.

In an instant, he dropped the gun and got on the ground, face down. A fellow officer had heard me yelling the commands and found me. At that point, the suspect complied with every command, and he was taken into custody.

For the next few days I remember replaying that situation over and over in my mind. What could I or should I have done differently, better? While I had drawn my service weapon many times before that, this was the first time I had pointed it at another human being knowing that I could and would take his life. It wasn't just that thought that struck me.

Had he chosen differently, I would have chosen differently, and both of our lives would have been changed forever. It was also the realization of the enormous responsibility that comes with taking the oath and wearing the badge. Every choice and decision I made as a police officer had a direct impact on someone's life. Decisions we make as police officers can and are life-altering, not just for the people we encounter, good and bad, but also for ourselves.

I never again took that authority and responsibility lightly.

When I see the actions of police officers scrutinized in the media, I think back to that day. If you've never been a police officer, if you've never been in that situation, if you've never been faced with making a split-second decision like that, you don't know. And you can't know.

A few years later, I became a field training officer teaching new recruits and then transferred to our department's Training Unit. I was promoted to sergeant in 1985 and served as a field training sergeant until my transfer to the Criminal Investigation Division in 1988.

Post-Hurricane Andrew

I was initially assigned to the Property Crimes Unit as the supervisor. I began attending as many training classes as I could, and after a few years, I was transferred to the Sex Crimes Unit.

In 1992, while in the Sex Crimes Unit, Hurricane Andrew hit South Florida. The devastation caused by its landfall in Homestead was overwhelming. Assistance was requested, and the city of Tallahassee responded. With the city providing utility services to its citizens, they put together a large convoy of utility workers, equipment, and trucks to respond to Homestead. They requested TPD officers travel with them and provide security as things were still unstable in the South Florida area.

I was asked if I would go along with two other officers. There was no power in that area and wouldn't be for some time, so securing lodging wasn't possible. We each had to find our own place to stay. I had friends a little further north in Miami Lakes, and the other two officers had family in the area.

Growing up in Florida and on the east coast, I considered hurricanes a part of life. When Tallahassee took a direct hit by Hurricane Kate in 1985, I worked an extended period of time without days off and personally went without power for almost three weeks. But the devastation I saw in Homestead caught me off guard.

We arrived in South Florida two days after Andrew made landfall. There is something unforgettable about seeing an eighteen-wheel tractor trailer embedded in the side of a building, propelled by the sheer force of Mother Nature.

With travel time, we worked fourteen hours every day. The United States Navy had set up a kitchen at a nearly demolished fast food restaurant. They fed all relief workers or provided MRE's (Meals, Ready-to-Eat). While we appreciated having food, the other officers and I were able to make different arrangements. I stopped at a large chain grocery store in Miami Lakes early each morning to pick up a sandwich, snacks, and drinks and fill my cooler with enough to get me through the work day.

My first day working in Homestead provided a challenge that I was not prepared for. I was approached by a young man who didn't speak English. While we couldn't verbally communicate, he showed me a very nasty wound on the inside of his upper thigh. He finally turned and pointed down a side street, and there I saw a large dog. There happened to be some military troops in the area, and one soldier came up to me and said that the dog was quite aggressive and had bitten this man.

Radio communication was spotty among myself and the other officers with me. I walked with the soldier down the street, looking for a possible owner. The dog was indeed aggressive, charging at me and anyone in the area. As it charged again, I drew my service weapon and shot the dog. I had dogs of my own at the time and always have. I hated that was the only recourse I had. The majority of officers work their entire career without having to fire their service weapon. Luckily for me, that is the only time I had to do so.

Over the next few weeks, I developed a renewed appreciation for my fellow first responders and for our utility workers. Officers from local agencies would check on us and thank us for being there. They were driving marked and unmarked police vehicles. Most of the windows had been blown out. Some wore a uniform shirt and jeans, others whatever they had that identified them as a police officer. They had no power in their own homes to launder their uniforms, and some had lost everything. But here they were, working to help their communities while their families were dealing with their own recovery issues.

Our utility crews worked hard. It wasn't long before they ran out of all the materials they had brought with them from Tallahassee. Thankfully, their supervisor was not an idle man. He sent groups out to find downed and damaged power poles to recover useable parts and pieces. Long work days of hard, physical labor in August in the South Florida heat and humidity were not easy. As I said earlier, I quickly developed a renewed sense of appreciation for them and the work they did.

We worked in Homestead for three weeks. We were relieved by a fresh group of officers and allowed to go home. I never again complained about having to work during or after a hurricane, and to this day, I never complain about going without power for a few days. I take preparation seriously and make sure our portable generator is working, that it has plenty of fuel, and that we have several propane tanks so that we can cook on the grill, just to mention a few things.

Sex Crimes

It was in the Sex Crimes Unit that my outlook on police work once again evolved. The loss of property can be and is often traumatic for those who suffer that loss. But crimes against a person are very different. As a patrol officer, you work the initial scene, and you move onto the next call, no matter how gruesome or traumatic it was.

As a detective, you often are called to the initial crime scene but are then tasked with conducting the follow-up investigation. This includes interacting with the victims and their families, often for days, weeks, or possibly years depending on how the case progresses through the criminal justice system. You relive that crime over and over. You are often the only voice victims or their families have.

In 1994, I was transferred to the Homicide Unit, where I worked for ten years. The thought of being the only voice that victims had was heightened. I also supervised the Victim Advocate Unit, which was staffed with four full-time advocates. We called them first-responder advocates because they worked on call just like the detectives, and they often responded to active, gruesome crime scenes. Many law enforcement agencies don't have a fully staffed Victim Advocate Unit; we were fortunate. They were an invaluable part of the team, but most people don't know they exist, unless you need their services. For me, they will always be a part of the Village of First Responders.

Homicide detectives are often main characters in television shows and in films, and that's the perception people have of the job. But it's nothing like that. You don't show up on a scene, look around for a few minutes, determine the time of death, know immediately what type of weapon was used, identify a suspect, locate that suspect, interview them, arrest them, go to trial, and convict them...in one hour. I wish!

During my time in the Homicide Unit, I was on call twenty-four hours a day, seven days a week. I was required to be available to respond to all homicides and any other type of death or violent crime that another supervisor deemed appropriate. For a seventeen-month stretch, I was also given the joint Leon County Sheriff's Office/Tallahassee Police Department Robbery Task Force. I was responsible for three units and fourteen employees. Fifty- to sixty-hour work weeks weren't that uncommon, and I would often go weeks without a full day off.

There was one particular stretch of time when I had been called out several nights in a row. The on-call detective called me at home and woke me from a sound sleep. He told me he was on a scene with four individuals who had been shot, and he needed me to respond. I told him to give me a few minutes, and I'd be on my way.

The phone rang again; this time it was one of our dispatchers. He told me the detective I had spoken to earlier wanted to know if I was coming. I said, "Of course. Is there a problem?" The dispatcher hesitantly told me, "He called you about thirty minutes ago, and you haven't called in service and en route on the radio." I was so exhausted that I fell back asleep. My response wasn't appropriate enough to put in this story, but we all still laugh about it.

For the detectives, they rotated being on call. When on call, they worked an afternoon shift and were available for any major incident after normal business hours until eight the following morning. They worked ten days straight then had four days off.

I'm happy to hear things have changed at my old department. There are more detectives and supervisors, and the on-call schedule is vastly improved.

The Reality of an Investigation

When I tell people that what they see portrayed on television and film is not a true depiction of what homicide detectives do, they get curious and want to know what it is really like. This is not meant to be graphic; it is reality.

They respond to crime scenes that are often bloody and gruesome, and at times spend hours there with the crime scene technicians. Some crime scenes take more than one day to process.

They are exposed to every possible way a human can die and in all stages of decomposition, from recently deceased bodies, to bloated bodies, bodies covered in maggots, bodies that have been dismembered and disemboweled, bodies that are mummified, or merely skeletal remains.

They help search for body parts, and collect body parts. They wear full body, fluid repellent, bio-hazard suits and gas masks. They attend autopsies; not just for a few minutes, but from start to finish. These often take hours. They get notified days after an autopsy that the victim had an infectious disease and that they were exposed to it and needed to be tested and monitored.

They conduct hours of interviews with witnesses and suspects. Based on a myriad of factors, they then have to determine if they are telling the truth. They pore over physical evidence and have some of those things sent to the state crime lab for additional forensic testing.

They write reports and prepare full case files for the prosecutor's office. They attend depositions and testify in courtroom proceedings. They deal with family and friends of the victim.

They often work past exhaustion. They miss countless family functions and have many sleepless nights. I could recount many crime scenes to drive home those points but will only mention one. Workers clearing a ditch with a backhoe dug up a partial body that was quite decomposed. After hours on scene looking for remaining body parts, I requested that someone from the Medical Examiner's Office respond. What we had located was transported to the morgue, but they wanted us to continue to search, as locating the head was crucial in identifying the remains.

They left the scene, and the detectives, crime scene technicians, and I continued our search for hours with the help of the backhoe operators. Eventually, we located the head. We preserved it appropriately, and I placed it in the back seat of my unmarked police vehicle. I drove it to the morgue and transferred custody to the Medical Examiner.

Just think about that for a moment. I'm driving in an unmarked police vehicle with a human head on the floorboard of the backseat, directly behind my driver's seat. Not only was I praying that I didn't get into a traffic accident on my way to the morgue, but knowing this was someone's family member, I wanted nothing more than to be able to identify this person. Sadly, we never did.

The Need for Closure

I've asked everyone in my books to tell me what the most difficult part of their job is or was. For me, it was not being able to bring closure to families, no matter how hard we tried. When people questioned the veracity of our work or stated that we didn't care if we solved a case or not, that hurt. That wasn't how we worked.

During my time in homicide, I began to question my faith. I saw up close and personal what we as humans can do to each other. How could God, any God, allow those things to happen? Eventually, I reached this conclusion: everyone is born with the power of choice, a gift. It's up to each person to make the most of that gift. Some choose wisely, and some choose poorly.

Dealing with the death of children was a bigger challenge for me. Over time, my only recourse was to try to not ask why but to believe there was truly a bigger plan that I was not privy to. The logic of the mind and the emotions of the heart were often an internal battle, but as with all first responders, you keep going.

It's difficult for me to describe what part of my job was my favorite or most rewarding. I suppose just the opposite of the above, to be able to bring closure to families and friends. But one of the things I loved the most was the teaching part, teaching new officers and helping new detectives learn and hone their skills, proudly watching them earn promotions and move onto bigger things.

I absolutely loved teaching at our Citizen's Police Academy and speaking to civic groups. I guess that falls in line with my passion for writing these books. People really don't know, but want to know.

I have some thoughts I want to share with those still working in the law enforcement profession. It isn't an easy job, and I know that. I know what you face and deal with every day. Be true to yourself, and do what you know in your heart is right, always. While it is an old cliché, it still rings true – treat everyone with respect; it's a two-way street.

And know this; there is life after law enforcement. But prepare for it; it is a huge change. Working in the Homicide Unit for ten years, I became the face of it. I did interviews for our local television stations. I would brief city officials on major crimes. At times I would get stopped in the grocery store and asked, "Aren't you…?" I didn't realize it, but I had become Homicide Sergeant Donna Brown.

Stay Grounded

I finally reached a point and had an epiphany of sorts. It brought me back to reality; I wasn't Homicide Sergeant Donna Brown; that's what I did for a living; it was just my job. I had lost myself; I had lost just being Donna Brown. Don't do that. Stay grounded, and don't let the job consume you. Again, stay true to yourself.

A few months into my retirement, I found myself pacing one day. Not a panic attack, but I'm not sure I can accurately describe it. It finally dawned on me... I had NO stress in my life! I was no longer tethered to two cell phones, a home phone, a pager, and a police radio. I could actually put a book on my nightstand; it was no longer cluttered with electronic devices. Oh, what a moment that was, and I haven't looked back.

For those who have never worked in law enforcement, I offer you this: most people only see a badge; behind and beyond the badge is what you need to know – the person. Do I believe that one hundred percent of all cops are good? No, I don't. But that's no different from any other profession. Overwhelmingly, the majority of cops are good cops, but more importantly, they are good people. They are no different than you; they just put on different work attire than you do.

When an issue comes to light in the media, please remember that things are not always as they seem. There is often more to the story than what has been presented. Please don't jump to conclusions without all the facts.

My books don't have the power to change minds, but perhaps by offering a different perspective, I can open them.

My professional life was an incredible journey, and I want to thank all first responders for your service, especially those who allowed me to share that journey with them. Each and every one of you will always be family and hold a special place in my heart.

Sergeant Scott Angulo

**Tallahassee Police Department
Active Duty: Sixteen Years of Service**

When I first approached Scott about letting me tell his story, he was very hesitant. His wife had purchased the first *Behind and Beyond the Badge* for him, and he had not finished reading it. We talked about why I wrote the book and why I wanted to include him in Volume II. He told me that he wanted to finish the first book and then get back in touch with me at that point.

Some people whom I approach about the book are hesitant to get involved for their own personal reasons, and I respect those reasons. Scott was hesitant, but I sensed his hesitation went beyond personal. When he finished reading the book, we spoke again, at great length. He told me that he very much wanted to be involved and how he liked the intent of my books. There were some logistical points to work out, which took some time, but together we overcame them.

With each of our conversations, I thought I was beginning to understand his hesitations and concerns. I asked Scott to put some of his thoughts on paper and send them to me. When I read them, I realized I had been totally wrong in my previous assessment.

As someone who did the job for twenty-six years, I know the far-reaching effects this profession can have on individuals and their families. Or so I thought. I'm honored that Scott agreed to let me tell his story, as he truly opened his heart.

Scott was born and raised in Tallahassee, Florida, and his family has been in that area for four generations. He said, "Being a cop was always on my radar. I went through phases of wanting to do other things as I got older. I started college as a computer science major, and later on, I took medical classes; however, I always seemed to come back to law enforcement.

"I am who I am because of my parents. My dad was raised in the San Joaquin Valley of California, and worked in the fields from a young age along with my aunts, uncles, and grandparents. I grew up hearing about hard work and sacrifice. My father was the hardest working man I knew as a kid. He was always working and always successful at every job he had. I learned a strong work ethic from him. He's always working on something. I wanted to be like him when I grew up.

"My mother was a stay-at-home mom until I was in middle school. She always impressed upon me the need to take care of others, especially those in my charge.

"My Uncle Lou is another influence that led to my career choice. He worked at the Tallahassee Police Department (TPD) for over thirty-five years, most of it in vice. I heard him tell war stories and saw the pictures of big drug busts. I wanted to do that.

"I studied judo for a while under a TPD sergeant in the basement of the police station. Then for a short period of time, I joined the Police Explorers, a group for kids interested in a career in law enforcement. I knew that police work was what I wanted to do."

Scott attended Florida State University while working full-time. He took a full course load of classes and started a family. He earned his bachelor of science degree in criminal justice and a certificate in public administration.

"I did other jobs and always talked about applying to TPD and the Leon County Sheriff's Office (LCSO), but I never got around to it. Then 9/11 happened. That, coupled with a study that showed TPD had a staffing shortage of fifty officers, was the catalyst for me to apply."

Scott was hired by TPD and graduated from the police academy in 2002, at the top of his recruit class. Like the majority of new officers, Scott began his career as a patrol officer and eventually became a field training officer in charge of training new recruits.

He was transferred to the Criminal Investigation Division (CID) where he spent time in the Fraud Unit, Property Unit, Burglary Unit, and the Special Victims Unit.

When asked about the moment he feels defined his career, Scott had two responses. Both occurred while he was working in CID, a time period in which Scott's and his family's lives were changed forever.

The first incident occurred while Scott was working in the Special Victims Unit. An incident was reported to the police department that involved a student athlete from one of the local universities. This student was accused of sexual battery. After a lengthy investigation involving more than just TPD, the student was not charged. A documentary was made, and it received national attention.

Scott said, "In reference to this incident, I'm hesitant to talk much about it because I'm still the target of many people. I'll get random hate messages, emails, or even phone calls, and

I know someone just watched the documentary. I hate that I'll be known as the investigator from that case because of the stigma it carries. What bothers me about that case is that every sort of negative connotation that could be conceived was presented by the press and other people and was wholeheartedly believed. I wasn't allowed to tell my side of the story. At this point, I'm not sure I want to tell it because it'll only rehash things.

"As the incident was unfolding, I was being cast as a heartless, classless, corrupt cop who put a sports program above the alleged victim of a crime. I had to remain quiet as it was still an open, active investigation.

"After the investigation ended, I came to the realization that I had to continue to remain quiet because the longer the incident stayed on the news, the greater the possibility a victim may hesitate to come forward. I had several people, who knew the truth about my involvement, tell me I should come out swinging and maybe file a lawsuit on people who were making up things. My wife also wanted me to fight back, but when I told her why I didn't want to cause more controversy, she cried. She totally understood my position and my pain.

"I had worked my whole career sacrificing my time, my body, and my sanity to some degree, to have it all cast aside by people who didn't know me. People who had an agenda to push their own slant on me and the investigation wanted controversy because they didn't like sports teams, the police, or both.

"Even when it was pointed out that I had arrested and investigated several other athletes, some of whom were extremely well-known at the time of the arrest, I was still painted as a bad person. The media didn't care about that because it was counter to their agenda.

"I thought my deposition in the civil litigation against the university would put the controversy to rest. I had an attorney involved in the litigation shake my hand at the end and tell me I had done a good job and that he hadn't realized some of the facts of the case, especially early in the case.

"He said, 'You definitely didn't deserve the beating you took in the media.' He admitted he had relied on media reports about my involvement with this particular university and how that tainted his perception and actions. When he found out I wasn't a fan of college sports, much less a 'super booster,' he felt much better about how the case was handled. Most of the information reported in the media was simply not true.

"I still receive emails, phone calls [work and personal], and Facebook messages calling me everything imaginable and threatening to rape my wife and kids so that I could see how it feels.

"This case directly impacted my handling of the second incident, a shooting."

Scott said, "My day started out very simple and uneventful. I had been out in our driveway preparing my new truck [new to me] to be undercoated. I had my earphones on and was listening to music.

"It was a Saturday, and there was a home Florida State University (FSU) football game. I walked into the house to get ready because I had to work the game. Staffing is huge for these games, and all area law enforcement agencies have to provide personnel for security and traffic details. I put my uniform on the bed and gathered my badge and nametag to put on it.

"About that time, my son came into the room and said he saw two deputy cars drive down the road. I looked up and saw their vehicles parked near a house that had frequent problems. I thought it was just a continuation of those issues. I turned to go back to what I was doing when I heard gunshots. I then remembered an intelligence bulletin concerning a subject that lived up that road making threats to harm police officers.

"I looked at my wife, and she called the kids [ages nine, seven, and five] to her. I said they needed to go into the bathroom with Mommy because I had to go to work. I went to the safe and got my pistol and rifle out. My rifle magazines were already in my car. As I ran out the door, it hit me that other officers and deputies may not recognize me as a law enforcement officer as I had not yet put on my uniform. I then grabbed my exterior vest carrier and put it on that would identify me as the police. Elizabeth, my wife, came out of the bathroom and helped me strap that on as I put my handgun on my belt.

"The whole time I was getting my gear on, I heard gunshots, several of them. As I approached the door, I saw a firetruck arrive. It appeared to immediately take gunfire. The firefighters jumped out of it and ran into a ditch and up the road out of sight.

"I ran to my car and grabbed three rifle magazines and my police radio. I then started toward the sound of gunshots. As I moved along the west side of the road, I could hear occasional shots. It was then that I saw the first deputy.

"He was exhausted; he had been engaged in a gun battle with the suspect for a few minutes by now. He was obviously hurt.

I called to him and raised my arms so that he could see the word 'Police' on my vest. I yelled, 'I'm with you, brother. Where is he?' He nodded and motioned up the road. He was having trouble breathing. I then called him over to me. As he moved, I covered him. I didn't see anyone but did see a house on fire and auto glass from a bullet-ridden car in the roadway.

"Once the deputy got to me, I asked if he was okay. He said he had been shot in the back. I saw the hole in his shirt, but thankfully, he was wearing his bulletproof vest. I tried to reassure him that he was going to be okay. I really wasn't sure as I didn't know how this was going to play out or end. I asked him for a description, which he gave me. I started trying to see if I could find the shooter.

After a while [I don't know how long; time was really warped], I became aware of radio traffic about people coming to the area. I got on the radio to let them know I was on the scene. The descriptions were all over the place: male, female, uncertain on race. I was concerned there may be more than one shooter.

"The dispatcher advised that the suspect was looking into the deputy's car. I moved out toward the roadway to see if I could see the suspect, and I saw the car but no person. I moved back toward cover with the shot deputy, and then I saw the suspect for the first time - a white male.

"He came out between two vehicles and fired at me. I tried to fire back, but my rifle only made a clicking sound. My training clicked in. I attempted to clear the malfunction. The charging handle felt bogged down. I then removed the magazine and inserted another one as the deputy and I rushed to another cover, falling back to create distance and time.

"I stopped at a tree and came back on target. I looked around, expecting the shooter to emerge from around the corner of the house, but he didn't. I then had a feeling he might try to flank or attack me from the side through the backyard of a house. The only 'cover' I had here was a privacy fence with gaps in it. The wounded deputy and I then moved to the corner of the neighbor's house. The deputy looked in the direction where we had seen the suspect while I searched to see if he was flanking us. I continued to check my rifle to make sure it wasn't still inoperable.

"I had a feeling of determination and focus unlike I've ever had before. I don't remember very many specific thoughts other than I had to win this; he hurt one of us. He tried to kill us.

"I then heard a vehicle come into the area and recognized it was another TPD officer. I tried to tell him I had just seen the suspect in the direction he was headed. Just then I heard three gunshots from the area where I last saw the guy. I knew where he was.

"As I moved from cover to go that way, I saw movement. It was the shooter looking around the corner. I stopped and stepped back to the corner of a house. I saw him peek again, this time lower. He then came out and moved laterally toward a tree. Gunshots were exchanged between the suspect and myself, and he fell.

"About a minute later, I was glad to see the other TPD officer was okay. The two of us converged on the suspect and attempted to render aid; however, a paramedic who had arrived on scene declared him dead.

"I looked around and saw the chaotic scene. My training again kicked in. I saw people arriving and walking all over the crime scene. I asked who had crime scene tape and then started directing tape to be put up. I was explaining what had happened to those in charge of the investigation. I then realized that my rifle and I were physical evidence, so I stepped aside and let those who had arrived do their jobs.

"From there, everything seemed very surreal. Thinking back, it still feels like it was a bad dream. Since the crime scene had become the house across the street, I walked back to my yard to tell my family I was okay and that I was in for a long day. After speaking with my wife for a few minutes, I walked back toward the scene. I was amazed at the number of officers and firefighters. I didn't want to re-enter the crime scene, so I started walking to a ditch culvert across the street.

"Then I saw a Leon County Sheriff's Office Deputy, who must have been in one of the two deputy cars driving down my road while I was getting ready for work earlier. I learned his name was Deputy Chris Smith, and he was lying in the road. Until that moment, it didn't hit me that a deputy had been killed. I'm sure I had heard it on the radio, but it didn't sink in until I saw him. The memories of the radio traffic transmissions came back to me all at once.

I told the officer who had been assigned to stay with me, that I needed to sit down, and that my chest hurt. He pushed me back and started checking me to make sure I hadn't been shot. I couldn't sit still and began pacing around in the roadway.

"Soon after the incident, Elizabeth called my parents to come pick up the kids. They didn't need to see what was happening.

"I was taken to the station to be interviewed. I was photographed, and my firearms were taken and impounded after their magazines were emptied and rounds counted. I met with my appointed attorney, and we agreed to be interviewed that day.

"For the four years previous to this incident, I was an investigator. I had interviewed dozens upon dozens of people in the interview room. Every time I sat on the same side of the table. This time I was sitting on the opposite side, the 'suspect' side. This seemed a little surreal as well.

"Then the investigators came in and read me the Miranda warning. It's a sobering experience to have your rights read to you. I gave the interview, and upon walking out of the interview room, was given papers placing me on Administrative Leave and directing me to go see a psychiatrist.

"I was taken home, and my wife was there. I really couldn't, and still struggle to put into words, my feelings at that time. I was extremely happy to see her and was comforted to be home; however, I had a very empty feeling inside.

"Elizabeth and I spoke for a while, but not about the incident, just about the command vehicles and officers in the yard and in the street. She then suggested we walk to church where we could unwind in a quiet place without the views and sounds of what was going on at home.

"Our house at the time had a very large picture window that faced the street. Unless I was in a bedroom, I could see out that window. That evening, it consisted of no fewer than four command vehicles and dozens of officers and crime scene technicians walking around. I could also see the body of the man I just killed lying in the grass across the street. Luckily, a firetruck and command vehicles blocked my view of where I had found Chris lying in the street.

"I had a hard time wrapping my head around what had just happened. I had just spent a year in a nightmare and felt like it had just stepped up a notch. I felt like I couldn't talk to anyone about what I was feeling regarding taking a life and the emptiness that came with that. It was very lonely.

"We got to church, and confession was going on, but there were very few people. I seized that opportunity to talk to our priest about the empty feeling I had. Everyone I saw at the station was telling me it was okay, that I shouldn't feel guilty or bad for what I had to do. It made me feel broken because I didn't feel either.

"I had to know if I was broken. I went into the confessional and sat across from the priest. I told him I wanted to talk to him about something that had happened earlier. I then told him I had killed someone. He turned flush.

"I told him the story, and he listened. When I was done, he assured me I wasn't feeling bad or guilty because I knew in my heart I did what I had to do. I felt better about that, but something was still bothering me. I just couldn't put my finger on it.

"That night I had issues sleeping. All I could think about was whether I could have done more to save Chris and wondered about his family. These thoughts went on for a couple of days. Then I received a call from an investigator working the shooting with a follow-up question.

"Despite being told by my attorney and TPD not to speak to anyone about the case after the interview was complete, I had to get answers to my questions. He told me there was nothing anyone could've done to save Chris. It was a planned setup by the suspect, an ambush. He had set his own home on fire and then called 911. He was going to kill any police officer or first responder who arrived. That's why he also shot at the fire truck when it arrived. I was able to sleep for a few hours that night.

"I was then asked to attend a candlelight vigil for Chris at the FSU baseball field. When I arrived, I got word that they may want to recognize me and have me sit on the stage with the community leaders. The thought of this troubled me. I felt the vigil should be completely about Chris. I made myself scarce and watched from the stands.

"The next day, I was told Chris' family wanted to meet me at his funeral. I was humbled by the invitation. Upon arrival at the church, I was greeted by command staff members from both my agency and from the Leon County Sheriff's Office, Chris' agency. I was then led to Chris' widow. I had no words for her; all I could do was say I'm sorry. I wanted to say more, but truly what could I say? She has been amazing through this. To have to relive losing Chris over and over with every award, with every anniversary or dedication, has to be beyond difficult. She's done it with grace, and I admire her strength. I don't know that I could be that strong if I lost Elizabeth.

"Since I worked in investigations, I was allowed to return to work in a limited capacity, about two weeks after the incident.

"Three months after the incident, I was asked to attend the grand jury that had been convened in reference to the shooting. In our jurisdiction, this is common practice. I testified before the grand jury, and they determined it was a justified shooting. This was a huge relief because I was sure something negative was going to be decided after all the heat I took in the previous incident. After being the target of media ridicule for a year, I wasn't sure what was going to happen after this. I was convinced there was no way they were going to let me out of this in a good way. I knew I did nothing wrong, but I couldn't help but think it was just a matter of time before it all came crashing down on me.

"Then the awards started. I received:

- The Congressional Badge of Bravery
- The International Association of Chiefs of Police (IACP) Officer of the Year
- Tallahassee Police Department Medal of Honor
- Leon County Sheriff's Office Medal of Valor
- Florida Police Chief's Association Officer of the Year
- The VFW National, State, and Local Awards
- American Police Hall of Fame Silver Star of Bravery
- Committee of 99 Officer of the Year
- Tallahassee Police Department Commander in Chief's Award

"Every time I received an award, I felt awkward. I thought it was odd to be awarded for doing what I was trained to do. I spoke to an officer, who I considered to be a mentor, about the award ceremonies. They told me to think of them as honoring Chris.

"Before the incident, I had already read articles and books written by officers involved in shootings. Most had similar reactions to the aftermath. They often write about sight, sound, and smell triggers. They talk about how difficult returning to the scene and anniversaries are.

"My situation was different than most because of my house's large picture window. Every day when I woke up or walked out of the house, I was returning to the scene. The suspect fell in the front yard directly across the street from my house.

"I found myself getting adrenalin dumps for a while afterward. It happened about a week after the incident when I was at the Boy Scout camp and smelled a .556 being shot. It happened again during an in-service training class. While teaching malfunctions, two of the instructors yelled 'fix it, fix it.' Hearing that triggered an emotional response, and at that moment, I remembered hearing those voices in my head saying those same words when my rifle malfunctioned the first time on the scene.

The Ripple Effect

"My family was also affected. As I said earlier, my wife took the kids to the master bath to hunker down. She told me about hearing the gunshots ring out and the kids hysterically crying as they prayed. My daughter cried out at one point, 'Is my daddy going to die?' There was a couple-minute lull in the sounds, and Elizabeth came out to see what was happening. My son, Vincent, followed.

"As they entered the living room, they looked out the large window and saw the man peering around the house across the street. They saw him run out from behind the house to engage me, and they saw him fall to the ground from being shot. They watched him roll on the ground in agony until we got to him, and then they saw the paramedic pronounce him dead and be blocked with a screen. Elizabeth stated she could hear him moan in agony and me yelling commands at him to drop the gun.

"Because of what the youngest kids saw, we took them to a counselor. At the time, the two youngest seemed to have no issues. When asked about horrible or scary events they've seen or experienced, they talked about bees in the yard.

"My second oldest, however, had issues reconciling the incident in his head. He was hyper-vigilant. Anytime he saw a police car or a firetruck, he would get anxious and visibly sick. He would beg to leave the area. If he heard sirens, he would compulsively ask where we thought they were going. He went to a counselor a few times, but we quit when it was suggested he not be exposed to 'police stuff.' As anyone on the job knows, police work is a way of life; it's impossible to escape 'police stuff'.' I wear a gun and badge every day, I drive a police car, and it sits in our driveway.

"I was fortunate to be invited to a COPS (Concerns of Police Survivors) retreat in Missouri. While there, I got to speak to a counselor who works with kids with PTSD (Post Traumatic Stress Disorder). She suggested we get an item he enjoys, and when he gets anxious, bring out the item and talk about pleasant things to break his focus. She stated pets are good for this as it can be soothing to pet a dog. We took her advice and adopted a rescue dog. It made a huge difference but didn't end all of the issues.

"Every now and then, the youngest two would bring up the incident and talk about it or ask a question, but once the comments were addressed or questions answered, they'd let it go. My daughter would routinely say, 'I'm glad that bad guy didn't kill you.' They developed issues with where we lived. They wouldn't play outside alone, and the younger two had to have someone in their rooms at night.

"They seemed to be recovering, and time was helping; however, in July 2017, I reached my breaking point with the constant exposure to the scene and what it was doing to the kids. An elderly man up the road, about where the incident started, had a heart attack. Sheriff's cars, firetrucks, and ambulances all responded to the area. All three of the youngest kids were on the verge of a full-blown panic attack.

"They were pacing and frantically asking what was happening and all begged me not to go outside this time. The next morning, I called a realtor friend of mine, and we started the process to sell the house.

"We sold the house and moved to a nearby, much smaller town. The move was a life-changer. From the night we moved in, the kids played in the yard without hesitation, and all slept in their own rooms. They did, however, make sure to tell every new neighbor we met that we moved because 'Daddy had to shoot a bad guy at our old house.'"

"Elizabeth was solid throughout the incident and beyond. She was able to hold the kids together and support me throughout. I had no idea how distant I was afterward, and she didn't tell me because she said she knew I had to work things out. She told me that for about three months, every time she'd bring up the incident, I'd look at her [sometimes through her] and walk away. I have no idea why this happened, and I didn't realize it was happening.

"She did have one episode, about two years later. She loves to shoot, but we hadn't gone to the range since the shooting. However, we decided to go one day. We were at the range shooting, and she asked to shoot my rifle. I loaded it and handed it to her. She shot it once, then started crying. She said she didn't understand why, just that it was overwhelming and emotional to hear it being shot.

"On the anniversary of the shooting incident, a major media channel ran a documentary about the college sexual battery case. Their decision to air it went public about two weeks prior. Almost every day I got phone calls, Facebook messages, and emails. My wife got several, too. They weren't nice ones.

Moving Forward

"To this day, I'm uncertain how to explain how I feel about the incident. On one hand, I'm glad when the time came I could put my training in action; however, I also feel an unsettling kind of anger.

"I'm angry because I gave that man what he wanted. He planned the ambush. He knew he wasn't going to survive. He had a chance to tell people goodbye as he wrote a letter. He destroyed his house by setting it on fire, killed a great man, made sure people remembered his name, and was killed. He knew he was going to die that day. He wanted to die, and I gave him that.

"Chris arrived doing what God called him to do, help people. As he tried to do just that, he was murdered by a coward. He wasn't allowed to tell his family goodbye. They had to endure the pain of hearing the news, attending the funeral, and not having him there for the holidays. Now his family is without him, and for what?

"The perpetrator also took the innocence of my small children. I wish it was all just a bad dream."

In December 2016, Scott was promoted to sergeant and assigned to a patrol squad. He currently supervises a Community Oriented Policy and Problem Solving (COPPS) squad.

Scott has been a member of the Tallahassee Police Department's Honor Guard since 2003, and has been involved with the Police Unity Tour for the past five years. The primary purpose of the Police Unity Tour is to raise awareness of law enforcement officers who have died in the line of duty. The secondary purpose is to raise funds for the National Law Enforcement Officer's Memorial and Museum.

The Police Unity Tour was organized in May 1997, by Officer Patrick P. Montuore of the Florham Park Police Department. What started with eighteen riders on a four-day fund-raising bicycle ride from Florham Park, New Jersey, to the National Law Enforcement Officers Memorial in Washington, D.C., has grown into nine chapters consisting of nearly twenty-five-hundred members nationwide who make the trip annually.

Each year, a week in May is dedicated as National Police Week and is celebrated in Washington D.C. During that week, those officers killed in the line of duty the previous year are honored at a candlelight vigil attended by family members and friends, and their names are inscribed on the memorial walls. Thousands of people often attend this event.

In May 2014, Scott said that he was feeling burned out from the job and was considering a career change. TPD was gearing up for that year's Police Unity Tour, and one of the support team members had to back out. Scott was asked if could fill in as a driver for a support vehicle, and he agreed to go.

"This was my first casual contact with survivors of fallen officers. The entire week I met survivors and coworkers of fallen officers and heard their stories. Seeing the wall for the first time was awe-inspiring. I felt a renewed calling to the job. Then I had the honor of escorting survivors to their seat for the candlelight vigil. The temperature was very hot.

"The first survivor I was assigned to changed my life. I met her at the door to the bus that had transported her and others to the memorial. She was an elderly woman. I introduced myself and asked for the honor of escorting her to her seat.

"After looking at me for what appeared to be several minutes, she took my arm, and we began to walk. I re-introduced myself and asked her who she was there to honor. She said it was her husband and that he had been killed a long time ago, but that they were just now adding his name to the wall. He had been forgotten.

"As we walked some more, she looked at the patch on my uniform sleeve. She asked if I was from Florida, and I said I was. She then asked why I came to Washington D.C., and I told her to honor heroes like her husband.

"The woman replied, 'You never met him. You're not from my town, and you're here, away from your family for him?'

"I said, 'Yes, ma'am. He's my family too; your husband was a brother.'"

"She stopped and looked me in the face. 'You don't understand. No one back home cared, not then and not now, and now all of you are here, and you all care."

"I said, 'Yes, ma'am.'"

"She fell into me and began to cry. I did, too. At that moment, I knew I could never do any other job."

Leon County Sheriff's Office Deputy Christopher Smith, end of watch November 22, 2014. You will never be forgotten.

Scott, thank you for your service to your community.

Officer Deborah Powell

Jacksonville Sheriff's Office
Retired: Thirty Years of Service

One of the more difficult things about writing this book, as well as Volume One, was deciding who to include. There are so many wonderful first responders with amazing stories to tell. I was talking with a friend one day who strongly suggested I contact Deborah. I'm glad I did.

Deborah knew she wanted to serve her community in some capacity and initially thought that a career as a social worker would be her path. But three of her older brothers chose public service careers, and one persuaded her to do the same. One brother was a major with the Florida Marine Patrol, another a regional director for the State of Florida Division of Alcoholic Beverages and Tobacco, and the third worked as a corrections officer, a State Beverage Agent, and later a fire chief. All three honorably retired from their respective agencies. Public service was very much a part of Deborah's family, and another brother encouraged her to pursue a correctional officer position.

Corrections Officer

Deborah made several attempts to qualify for the city of Jacksonville's (Florida) correctional officer test, but she didn't meet the height requirement, which was six feet. The city eventually dropped the height requirement, whereupon Deborah took the test, and in 1974, became a correctional officer.

According to Deborah, "At that time, 1974, there was no academy in Jacksonville for correctional officers, so on my first day of work, I began on-the-job training and was assigned to the main jail. As police officers brought female prisoners in, the on-duty female correctional officer was called to the back door of the jail to receive the prisoner. We would see that person through the entire booking process and then to her cell. I remember wondering if I had made the right choice in leaving my previous job.

"My first few weeks were a real adjustment. I witnessed people being brought into the jail I never knew existed. Being raised in a single-parent, lower middle-income household, I realized I had indeed been sheltered from the underbelly of society. I had never seen anyone intoxicated to extreme levels. I had never heard profanity spouted as much as I did those first few days. But I knew securing this job would mean a great opportunity to begin my career in service, so I continued. After six months working in the jail, a new position opened up for the first work-furlough program, and I took the job. I stayed in that position until 1979."

Recruited as a Police Officer

In the mid-to-late 1970s, many law enforcement agencies were looking to hire more female officers; the city of Jacksonville was no different. Deborah recounted this story. "In 1976, two detectives came to my house one evening, which scared the heck out of me. I thought I had done something wrong at work, but they were there to recruit me for the position of police officer. The only female police officers at that time had been grandfathered in from civilian positions. I couldn't accept the challenge at the time because my husband and I were expecting our second child. Had I been able to, I would have been the first class that received all of the same training the male officers did." The previous females did not receive the same academy training as the men.

In 1979, Deborah received another visit, once again offering her a position as a police officer. This time she accepted. When Deborah completed the academy, she was the third African-American woman to do so and the fifth woman overall.

Deborah's first assignment was as a patrol officer working the south side of Jacksonville on a relief squad. This squad covered patrol beats when the regularly assigned officers were on their days off. For her, learning this large geographical area was a great challenge. At that time, officers were assigned their own vehicles that they could take home; however, the department was short on vehicles, so she was assigned to ride with a seasoned officer. Deborah added, "This officer had been with the department for five years, and we rode together for about a year. He willingly shared his knowledge, wisdom, and work experiences, and how he interacted with people was a great, positive example. For me, it was the cornerstone of my career."

Vice Unit
After two years on patrol, Deborah was "loaned" to the Vice Unit. She was recommended for this assignment by the same officer with whom she initially rode; he had been promoted to a detective position in the Vice Unit. This loan turned into a four-year assignment, the one she describes as her favorite position with the department. She said, "Vice proved to be a great assignment. There were so many things I never dreamed

I would get to experience: raids on homes and businesses where illicit drug activity had been documented and narcotics sting operations and surveillances that lasted for weeks. I loved it all.

"The unit had been investigating a large gambling organization but was unable to get someone on the inside. This investigation was why I was originally brought into the unit. They thought I might have a good chance of getting inside; they needed someone to actually 'make a bet.'

"Within a week, they established a deep undercover persona for me. I began showing up in the area, hanging out, and making acquaintances. I was finally able to place a bet with one of the main individuals, and we shut down what ended up being a large crime organization."

Deborah remained in the Vice Unit and worked with her mentor on other issues, including prostitution and indecent exposure problem areas. "We often had the highest arrest totals and clearance rates in the unit," she added.

Her mentor and partner transferred to another unit, and Deborah remained in the Vice Unit for another year. Crack cocaine had become prevalent in Jacksonville, and Deborah grew tired of undercover work. In 1986, she transferred back to the Patrol Division, where she remained until 1997. That year, she applied for and got a transfer to the Fugitive Unit.

Deborah enjoyed this position. "Our duties included not only locating and arresting local criminals, but we traveled all over the country, and at times outside the United States, to take custody of individuals who had been arrested in other jurisdictions on warrants issued in our area. The travel was extensive, and I had to be ready to go at all times. Sometimes we traveled by commercial airlines but also on the Sheriff's Department airplanes or helicopter. A great perk was that I got to go places I probably wouldn't have otherwise, like Puerto

Rico." Deborah remained in the Fugitive Unit for seven years until her retirement in 2004.

With the variety of assignments she had throughout her career, I asked Deborah to elaborate on her work schedules and the impact it had on her personal life. She said, "When I was on patrol, we rotated shifts each month. I would work seven a.m. to three p.m. one month, then three p.m. to eleven p.m. next month, then eleven p.m. to seven a.m. the following month. This schedule would repeat itself. It was difficult at times when also trying to raise a family. I was divorced, and being a single mother made it even more challenging. In the Vice Unit, I worked so many stakeouts and undercover assignments that my schedule was always changing.

"I was fortunate that my mother was near and helped out often with taking care of the kids. I always knew my kids were in good hands, which lessened the stress personally and at work. Words can't describe how much my mother's help meant to me over the years."

Hurricanes and Fires

While every first responder working in Florida has the potential to face natural disasters, that potential is often greater with hurricane season. Deborah worked during two hurricanes and described her duties this way: "We worked twelve-hour shifts and were told those could be longer, and all days off were cancelled. Our jobs varied but included monitoring flooding and closing roadways, monitoring downed powerlines, and assessing the overall damage. It was always difficult to leave your family, but you did your best to prepare your own home and family."

Deborah recounted a situation that involved a large fire started by an arsonist. The fire had been burning for about a week, and her squad was sent to the area to provide relief to the officers working it. She was given the task of checking two major roadways to assess if they were still safe for travelers or needed to be closed due to poor visibility.

When Deborah arrived at one roadway, visibility was clear, but that changed quickly. Winds shifted, and visibility became zero. "I couldn't see anything. My instant thought was that I might hit another vehicle or that I could be hit. The only option I had was to open my car door and shine my flashlight onto the roadway. I tried to stay close to the center line and notified headquarters of the conditions and my situation. The roadway was shut down until I could find my way out of the smoke. It took twenty minutes, but it was a long twenty minutes and a different kind of stress. The smoke smell in my hair, my clothes, my car, and in my nose is something I didn't soon forget."

I asked Deborah to tell me the most rewarding part of her career, as well as the most difficult. She said, "In the early part of my career, it was stressful to rotate shifts as often as we did. As soon as your body adjusted to that month's home and work schedule, it was time to change. I felt sleep deprived most of that time. But there were other issues I faced as well.

"When I was hired, the Jacksonville community was not used to female police officers, especially an African-American one. Racism was common. We weren't a welcomed addition to the department by the community or even other police officers. There were many times when I arrived on the scene of a call and the citizen would look at me and say they wanted a white officer. People would often challenge me, and the "N" word was commonly used. Things obviously got better, but it wasn't easy."

Deborah feels all of that was the most rewarding part of her career. "I always made sure I did what I was supposed to do and gave it my best. I treated everyone with respect, even though that respect wasn't always given back. I'm proud of that and my career."

Comforting a Dying Victim

When I asked Deborah if she had what she felt was a career-defining moment, she described this: "I was dispatched to a shooting incident one evening. When I arrived, the victim was lying in a pool of blood but still alive. I knelt next to him and tried to comfort him, at the same time asking him if he could tell me who did this to him. He was young, and I knew he probably wasn't going to survive. He tried to tell me something, but I couldn't understand what he was saying. Sadly, he died moments later.

"I was stunned. This was the first time I was the first officer to arrive on scene to this type of call. It was the first time I had witnessed someone die. This had a profound effect on me, seeing someone so young take their last breath. For the first time, I recognized my own mortality and just how fleeting life can be. I was a changed person; I had a new appreciation for life and family."

Deborah's family has always been important to her. As mentioned earlier, her mother was crucial in helping her balance a career and raise her children. As her children grew older, they began to understand the dangers of her job, and she would often hide injuries from them as she didn't want to add to their worries. Deborah describes her oldest child as becoming her "gatekeeper." She knew when Deborah needed to sleep, so she would keep her younger sibling entertained and wouldn't let anyone disturb her.

Now that daughter is married to a police detective who has served for twenty-five years with the Jacksonville Sheriff's Office (JSO). Her niece is also an officer with JSO and reached the rank of chief a few years ago. Deborah added, "Although I never made rank, I'm proud of our family's commitment to service in law enforcement."

I asked Deborah what she does now that she is retired. "As an officer, I always admired those people who found time to volunteer to help others. I promised myself that I would find a cause I could connect with and get involved. Three years after I retired, I had to have hip-replacement surgery. After my recovery, my surgeon asked if I would be interested in a new program they were starting. They wanted to pair patients who had undergone hip- or knee-replacement surgery with patients facing that same surgery. They would basically act as a mentor for these people. It was to be called 'The Joint Center.' I loved the idea and got involved working side by side with the physical therapists and the patients. I love it so much, and I've been doing it for seven years now."

Deborah still finds the time to play golf, something else she loves to do.

Thank you for your service to your community and keep enjoying retirement, Deborah. It's Phase 2 of your life, and you earned it.

Lieutenant James Fairfield

Watch Commander
Tallahassee Police Department
Active Duty: Twenty-Eight Years of Service

I have known James for many years, personally and professionally, and am good friends with his wife Tracy. I believe that is one of the reasons I asked him to let me tell his story. While the basic facts of his career mirror many, I find James to be a deep thinker, and he often provides an interesting perspective. Sometimes he even surprises me.

James earned his bachelor of science degree in criminology in 1989 from Florida State University and a master's in business administration in 1994. It is perhaps his minors that illustrate my earlier thought: They were in biology, English, and religion. As I've learned in writing these books, many law enforcement officers don't necessarily grow up wanting to be cops, and James is no different.

When I asked him why he chose a career in law enforcement, he said, "Historically speaking, growing up, I was probably more prone to run from the police than to them. I stumbled into the conflict between students in the variety of college classes I was taking. I found that my common sensibilities and sense of pragmatism felt better when associating with the criminology students who wanted to be police officers or join the military. I began resenting some of the business students who expressed a relentless pursuit of wealth, which kind of annoyed me."

While a full-time student at FSU and tending bar at night at a local establishment, James began working at the Florida Department of Law Enforcement (FDLE) in an entry-level position doing data entry and working in the mailroom. He had been told that this was a path to becoming an agent. He met several other individuals who had the same thought process, but they had been there for years. After nine months, he quit the FDLE job and concentrated on completing his degree.

Tactical Apprehension and Control Team

James was hired by the Tallahassee Police Department and graduated from the academy in 1990. When he was assigned to his first squad, his field training sergeant was a member of the Tactical Apprehension and Control Team (TAC), specifically the Entry Team (first through the door). TAC is the Tallahassee Police Department's name for their SWAT team. This sergeant was always a huge proponent of continued training. James said, "I realized I wanted more training and challenges. I felt TAC was a path for me." He spent his time working the streets, including two years as one of the department's first bike officers, a new community-oriented policing initiative.

He spoke with other members of the TAC team, asking questions, and in his words, "Gearing my physical training to the events I would face in tryouts for the team." James always believed in physical fitness and training and was a third-degree black belt in the Okinowan Uechi-Ryu form of karate. He added, "The tryout for TAC and the events are not like training for a triathlon, but they physically made for a long day, and openings on the team did not often become available. You had to have a good showing and win. On the day of the tryouts, I finished first in seven of the nine events and second in the other two. I still didn't get picked."

James continued. "I was crushed, but I masked it as anger." He talked to his first sergeant to find out why he hadn't been chosen even though he had done so well. The sergeant let him know that he couldn't "win" a position on the team and told him, "Everybody who tried out did well, but you have to do well in reality. Team members have to see you as an asset based on what you have done in reality, on the streets doing the job, not in a simulation."

"I worked with a few TAC members after that. It was a year and a half before another opening became available, and I could try out. This time I was selected. When looking back at my first tryout, I had only been a police officer for a few years and probably had no business being a part of the team with so little experience."

He said, "You find out quickly just how heavy all that gear you wear and carry really is. You find out how much fun the combination of Florida summers and wearing a gas mask for hours on end can be and just how boring it is to sit still in a van all night. TAC teams practice a lot, and those practices were usually hard. Running through clouds of chemical agents, along the tops of high-range walls, through the woods in total darkness; it was all part of the experience. But you realize what it's like to share that suffering for something bigger than a touchdown. Once you get to that point where you understand your mortality and how dependent you are on your team, you take it very seriously."

In 2002, James became the TAC Entry Team leader and served as the assistant team commander until 2012.

TAC is often visible in the media, on television, and in film, but few people truly understand its purpose. I asked James to explain. "Our TAC team had several missions that were defined in our policy manual, but the main mantra was always the preservation of life. Typically, that meant when something occurred that went beyond the capabilities of officers without specialized equipment and training, TAC was called.

"The most common situation encountered, we called the barricade. That doesn't mean somebody had fortified a location, although they sometimes did. It means somebody is inside a structure and will not come out. Many would say that any cop should be able to search a house. Yes, cops check houses and businesses after alarms and such. However, when they get information or believe the person inside is armed and knows we are outside, then you believe they are lying in wait with the advantage. Think about playing hide-and-seek when you were a kid. When you hid in your own house, you always knew when you were about to be found. Now play that same game with a gun. If you know you're about to be found, you always get the option to shoot first. That is a TAC game, not a patrol officer's game."

The TAC team also serves narcotics warrants, search warrants, and arrest warrants where violent people or weapons are involved. Add to that high-risk stakeouts, dignitary protection assignments, crowd control events, and hostage rescue. As the sergeant supervising the Homicide Unit, I would often call on the TAC team to serve some of our search and arrest warrants. I knew the target had already chosen to take a life and was not willing to put investigators at unnecessary risk. TAC was by far better equipped for those situations.

James explained in greater detail about hostage rescue scenarios. "Hostage rescue is different in that it is the only event where as a member of the team, you accept that you will put yourself in harm's way to create an opportunity to save the hostage. That's a big shift for officers. All the police training you get revolves around getting yourself home at the end of the day. Almost all of the TAC training you get is about a methodical application of tools and tactics to try and gain the advantage. Hostage rescue can be solved by a sniper shot, but if that opportunity does not present itself, then somebody will try to get themselves between the hostage and the suspect. If that's the task you draw, then you just hope somebody else on the team stops the suspect before he shoots you. Consciously surrendering yourself for the life of the hostage is a level of commitment most people don't understand. It's like the Secret Service agent who dives in front of the bullet; it's a bold thing."

There are different components to the TAC team, with the largest element being the Entry Team. There is also the Sniper Team, the Hostage/Crisis Negotiation Team, Explosive Ordinance Disposal Team, Tactical Medical Team, and the Logistics Team. Each has specific roles, but all work as one.

In 1995, the same year James made the TAC team, he was assigned to the department's training unit. He remained there for five years, earning a promotion to sergeant in 2000, then returned to working the streets. After three years as a field training sergeant, James was assigned to a unit that he considers his favorite of his career, the Career Criminal Unit.

Career Criminal Unit

The Career Criminal Unit worked very closely with the United States Marshall Service (USMS), a joint Violent Fugitive Task Force. As members of the task force, officers were granted status by the USMS to work outside their primary jurisdiction. For James and the members of his unit, that meant the availability to work outside the city limits of Tallahassee. Their main function was to locate and arrest violent offenders who had skirted apprehension. Local law enforcement agencies would submit warrants to the task force asking for their assistance with the arrest of these individuals. From the Homicide Unit perspective, I utilized their services and can personally speak to their effectiveness.

James was still on the TAC team and on call twenty-four hours a day, seven days a week, the same for the Career Criminal Unit and the task force. For a stretch of time, seventy-hour work weeks were not uncommon for him. This too can take its toll.

I've asked James to provide his thoughts on three other aspects of his career: the most rewarding part of his job, the most difficult, and what he considers to be his career-defining moment.

For the most rewarding part of his job, he said, "Foremost, I have had the chance to stand up for others. I had the chance to behave as if my life didn't matter more than someone else's. I have been able to suppress my 'self' in service to others, both citizens and officers. I have had a chance to make amends for the ignorance and selfishness of my youth.

What Cops Really Do

"Secondarily, now I know. I didn't know before. I know what cops really do and what they are thinking when they do it. I have seen the eyes and hearts and hands of others on the job. I know what really happens in the shadows. The papers, the pundits, the activists, the politicians have no clue. I know."

For the most difficult part of his job, he shared this. "When asked what you do for a living, the typical response for almost everyone is 'I am a ...' They seem able to clearly distinguish that their answer is what they do, not what they are. As a cop, there are times when the difference between who you are and what you do becomes fuzzy. I can't say if it's more profound for cops since I've never been anything else. There were some dark times when I couldn't be what I wanted to be at work anymore, and that ate into what I should have been at home.

"Certainly, I have been seriously hurt a few times. In general, wearing the gear around a waist that gets bigger and a back that gets weaker and stuffing that into a car that gets smaller every year can't be good for anyone.

"I can say that as I reach the twilight of my career, I carry the faces of the dead a bit longer than I used to. I can remember six or seven years ago on a TAC callout, deciding not to go into the room of a gunshot suicide where negotiations had failed. I knew what to expect. The man's dog – a Great Dane – had apparently been standing nearby and ran from the house after the shot. It was a very odd thing to see that giant macabre dog trotting around the perimeter, white with brown accents on one side and splattered red on the other.

"The decades prior to that, I would generally find myself there during the final clearing of a scene. I just decided I had seen enough. Well, that certainly wasn't my last. I think I have been back on the road on patrol less than ten months and have come upon at least a half dozen death scenes, mostly shootings, that I couldn't avoid. I see their faces for a few days 'til one is replaced by the next. I think what strikes me now is a sense of general sadness about what people do to each other and the reckless or ridiculous reasons they do it. That's probably just an aching 'dad bone'; it's the world my son has been shielded from, but not for much longer."

James couldn't recount a particular career-defining moment but talked about two incidents that certainly affected him both personally and professionally. As I mentioned at the beginning, I have known James in both capacities and consider him a good friend with bonds neither of us talk about much, but we know they are there. Cops are human.

Family and the job are intertwined for James as they are for many in the first-responder world. But I found his thoughts to truly be from the heart, so much so that I couldn't exclude them from his story.

James grew up in an unsettled home with his parents divorcing. He concluded that as an adult in a relationship, he would never do it this way. As a young police officer, he thought he would stay with the Tallahassee Police Department for five years or so and then with that experience, hopefully move on to a federal agency and eventually settle down and start a family. Then he met his future wife.

James told me, "She was a divorced single mother with a five-month-old son; this was absolutely not the situation I had planned. Yet, that is the path I took, and we were heading toward becoming an instant family." They weren't able to get married for a while as they were sadly faced with the worst of nightmares, a sick child.

Fighting Cancer with a Young Child

At almost twenty-two months old, Tracy's son Trevor became ill and was diagnosed with a brain tumor. James said, "There were the ups and downs of improvements and declines and the road trips around the country trying to find better news. It would be hard on any relationship, and many marriages don't survive it.

"Less than two years later, just before his fourth birthday, Trevor died. He was in his hospital bed, with me next to him. I wound up the little *Sesame Street* radio and let it play. His breathing slowed. He held my thumb, as he was prone to doing, and closed his eyes.

"I had thought a lot of things over that time and got as much good advice as bad. While he was fighting cancer, I was fighting with God, the bills, and sometimes Tracy. I had ignorant friends who would say 'At least he wasn't your biological son.' I would reply, with venom, 'Well, if your wife dies, at least she wasn't biologically related to you.' It wasn't their fault; there is no good thing to say. Many cops are socially awkward. Ultimately, I came to recognize that little boy was my greatest teacher, and he paid the ultimate tuition, not me. Loyalty, sacrifice, commitment, and love were all now more than words or concepts. I felt what it did to me and saw what it did to Tracy."

For James, "I've buried a few friends over the years, including one who was killed in the line of duty. But I consider burying Trevor probably the hardest moment of my personal life. Being at work allowed me to be in the moment and insulated me from the hardship at home. Danger kind of kept my attention off the sorrow."

I attended Trevor's funeral. A framed picture of him still sits on a table in our living room.

Tracy and James married almost one year to the day after Trevor died. Two years later, their son was born.

The Transformation to Lieutenant

The most difficult time in James' career, as close to a career-defining moment as he could explain, came with his promotion to lieutenant in 2012. It is very different from what most describe; a transformation of sorts.

I had been retired for several years when this happened. I knew how hard this was for James, but until now, I really didn't understand the effect it had on him. He explained, "Forced to admit it, the hardest point in my career came just after a promotion to lieutenant. I was, for a moment, the most senior sergeant in the department and could transfer pretty much anyplace I wanted. I didn't really want to go anywhere. I loved being in the Career Criminal Unit, but I was approached about advancing not just in rank but also the TAC team structure. I had been a sergeant for twelve years and had been essentially covering most of the active TAC command issues for the last three years.

"I know the saying goes, 'Be careful what you wish for,' but I was completely ambushed by the unforeseen. The illusion was that I was being promoted after eighteen years to assume the TAC team's command. I had it in my head that I had reached that point where I could turn in my heavy gear and guns on my own terms. I had lost a step or two but was still competitive in any drill or exercise we would endure. I was ready to go out without anyone having to remind me I was past my prime. To me it was the right time to now work to fix the organizational issues I had struggled against my entire tenure.

"That is not the way it went. I didn't see the background dealings. I was being promoted to lieutenant so another sergeant could move into my position. In reality, they had no intention of letting me move into the TAC Commander position. They had their own person they wanted in that position, another lieutenant. My advocates were told they were promoting me for the 'team,' but they too were misled.

"I panicked when I heard the rumors that I was being ousted. I called everyone of rank who would answer the phone, and nobody claimed to understand what happened. Some actually told me they had heard that I wanted to leave the team. Then I recognized the routine. This same group used the same tactic on a friend of mine a few years before.

"So there I was. I had lieutenant's bars, but the price I paid for those bars was the loss of the one thing that had kept me motivated and engaged in this profession—the TAC team; that had been my passion.

"I can remember trembling in rage when the new team phone list came out, and my name wasn't on it. I used to spend hours of off-duty time both physically training and developing props and lesson plans. The anger in my blood for those who did this to me spread like an infection. Tragically, that infection was suppressed at work but filtered its way into my home. I was detached and dejected. Instead of focusing that effort on something productive, I just lumbered around, absorbed in self-pity. I began flirting with dumb ideas to find adventure. In cop speak, that usually spells the end of a marriage or too much time with a bottle in your hand.

"It was more than two years before I came to the hard conclusion that this was not done *to* me. Agencies, entities, corporations, commanders very rarely do anything *to someone* as much as they are doing it *for someone*. You just feel that way if it's not you in the 'for' column. I got bumped to a day-shift office spot that was relentlessly boring and with predictable scheduling. As much as I felt like it was the icing on a terribly flavored cake, it turns out that was exactly what I needed to get my home, my family, and myself back on track. I like to say, finding my North."

The Effects on a Cop's Family

The effects on family members of those who are police officers, or any first responder, are real, but often they are left in the background, and it isn't talked about. James certainly has touched on this but wanted to go even deeper to explain to those outside his profession.

"The hardest transitions came when I would be reassigned, and the whole household routine would have to change." When talking about his promotion to sergeant, he said, "When I was promoted, I was assigned to second shift, often called afternoon shift. Our son was four months old. Three months later, I was moved to third shift, midnights. I spent about two years working the midnight shift. My friend and fellow TAC Team member, Sergeant Dale Green, was killed in the line of duty, and I was moved to the afternoon shift. It was bittersweet to move back to afternoon shift to fill the vacancy that his death created. After only six months on afternoon shift, I was moved back to midnight shift. I only mention the bouncing around as it was extremely difficult. It was the first five years of my son's life. Schedule changes don't just affect you but your spouse and your children as well. Even now, as I am working the afternoon shift, it's earplugs and sleep masks. Sometimes I go a couple of days without seeing my wife or son awake. That hurts me still."

James explained what happened one morning, "Tracy was up early. I had only been asleep a few hours, sleep mask and earplugs in place. I felt the cold steel of a gun's muzzle press against my head, and I exploded out of sleep mode ready to fight. It was cold, and she had been outside in the cold air. The gun was her nose as she kissed me goodbye. That hurts me too.

"So, for me now, after twenty-eight years as a police officer, there really is only my wife and son. I have many friends but no *best* one. Truthfully, I am selectively social. I'm not a recluse but can no longer deal with the crowds or throngs of people at a concert or large event. I can't isolate my family or protect them there. There's my work life and the cycle of people I trust with my life, and then the reason I think I am here, my family."

Missions for the Children

James is also involved in things outside of his work life. "I am an annual giver to the Make-A-Wish Foundation. I owe them a debt of gratitude for the trip they provided before Trevor died. I plan on paying them back for the rest of my life."

He is also an executive officer (Director of Projects) for a 501(c)3 non-profit organization called Orphan Logistics and Relief. James explained, "We have been on international outreach missions to El Salvador, Guatemala, and the Dominican Republic. I wish I could go twice a year. Most people have no idea what real need and poverty are. I know. These kids and people have nobody to call for help. They have almost no infrastructure and can't apply for federal aid, get free housing or phones. They just have to figure it out. I like that kind of person."

The initial goal of the organization was to build computer labs for distance learning at orphanages in these areas. They accomplished that on their first trip. On subsequent visits, once a volunteer anywhere on these compounds realized what they could do, they began getting requests to build other things: physical therapy stairs, media carts, baby changing stations, and storage cubes, to name a few. They've fixed wheelchairs, built shelves and beehives, and patched leaky roofs. His wife and son traveled and helped out on their last trip to the Dominican Republic.

I ask everyone if there are any thoughts, they'd like to pass onto other first responders or to those in the civilian world. Some answer; some don't. James told me he has thought about what many in the public believe about police officers: "That we beat people for no reason and then lie about it, steal from drug dealers, take bribes, harass and oppress certain members of the community." While he can't say that all cops are good cops, he will say the majority are. He proudly told me that if he were to take a polygraph test and was asked if he had ever done any of those things, he most certainly, proudly, without fear, could safely answer no. I believe him; he's one of the good guys.

James is eligible for retirement now but hopes to stay until the early part of 2020. He will reach mandatory retirement at that point with a little more than thirty years of service. But, he explained, "I used to joke years ago that if I became some overweight, coffee-sipping administrator sitting in an office, they would have to blast me into retirement with dynamite, but if I was still working a road shift and patrolling the streets, I would know to hang it up and get out before I got hurt. Yet here I am, twenty-eight years on the job and pulling second shift with all the new kids. 'Retirement' is a weighted word for me. I'm pretty sure I will do something productive once I leave. Having options is nice."

Thank you for your service to your community and for opening your heart. Your thoughts highlight the message that cops are human too.

Corporal Trish England

Traffic Homicide Investigator
Florida Highway Patrol
Retired: Twenty-Six Years of Service

Trish and I have been friends for more than fifty years. We grew up together in the small town of Titusville, Florida, went to the same high school, and moved to Tallahassee, Florida, to attend Florida State University. Our course of study and life after college took different paths, but we both ended up with careers in law enforcement.

Trish received a bachelor of science degree in 1978 and a master's degree in 1979, both in the field of leisure services and recreation administration from Florida State University. Most of the available jobs in this field were outside the state of Florida, and she really didn't want to travel or move from Florida. Without many options, she took a job with a large retail establishment where she stayed for two years.

A career in law enforcement was not a calling for Trish or even something she considered, then she learned that a friend's brother had applied for a job with the Florida Highway Patrol (FHP). After hearing this, she did some research and thought this might be an interesting career, not sitting behind a desk and a way to serve her community.

Florida Highway Patrol

She completed her employment application with FHP and was hired. She became a member of the Florida Highway Patrol Academy's sixty-eighth recruit class and graduated in 1983. At the time of her graduation, I had been with the Tallahassee Police Department for four years. The FHP Academy was in Tallahassee, and I attended her graduation. Those who knew us in high school would have never imagined!

Upon her graduation, Trish was assigned to Troop G and moved to Jacksonville, Florida. Troop G covered nine Florida counties, and she remained with them for the duration of her career.

She had several assignments over the course of her career, such as a field training officer for eighteen years tasked with helping train new troopers; she served on the community-oriented policing squad for three years, did undercover work targeting habitual DUI offenders for two years, and spent six years as a traffic homicide investigator. She was also a certified instructor in DUI enforcement, basic traffic homicide investigation, and photogrammetry, to mention a few.

When I asked Trish what her favorite position was, she said all of them. "I loved instructing, I loved training new troopers. I loved community-oriented policing, and I loved traffic homicide."

She didn't hesitate to define her least favorite position: undercover work. "I hated being in plainclothes and in an unmarked not-so-nice car. We'd sit for hours watching habitual DUI offenders' homes, just waiting for them to get behind the wheel of a car. Their driver's licenses had been suspended or revoked, yet we had received information that they were still driving. Stakeouts are not as glamorous as television and film make them out to be. It was like watching paint dry for days."

Like all law enforcement agencies, the Florida Highway Patrol has an active role in disaster response. Florida has its share of wild fires and flooding, but hurricanes are the most common events. With television crews everywhere and the prominence of social media, first responders are forefront in the response to such disasters. But few know what life is like for those who are out there.

Natural Disasters

When Trish was assigned to the Traffic Homicide Unit, she described her role in natural disasters or other special events. "We were assigned to twelve-hour shifts with other patrol units and on call when not on that shift. All our days off were cancelled as well as any previously scheduled vacation time. If the involved area was not your area of assignment, you were often told to pack a bag and sent to the affected area. You never knew for how long; sometimes it could be for weeks or sometimes for months.

"When we were sent to areas affected by a hurricane, the plan was usually for a two-week stay, but that wasn't always what happened; the stays could be longer. We would stay in hotels, many of which didn't have electricity or hot water. When working in these areas, trying to find a restroom was always a challenge too. Many of our troopers were sent to areas affected by Hurricane Katrina, and some had to sleep in their cars. Food was almost always cold and usually a box-type meal or a military MRE (Meals, Ready-to-Eat), not the best, but we were glad to have it. There was little contact with family at home as phone lines and cell towers were down. Laundry was done in bath tubs or sinks. We certainly didn't look our sharpest!"

Even if they were not actually deployed to an affected area, they still worked twelve-hour shifts with no days off to cover the staffing shortages in their area due to others being gone. These work schedules were also implemented for large events such as the Super Bowl.

Traffic Homicide Investigator

Of all the assignments Trish had with the Florida Highway Patrol, her six years as a traffic homicide investigator was by far the most difficult. The training itself to become a traffic homicide investigator is hard, but doing the job is also challenging mentally and can take its toll.

Trish explained, "Aside from the academy itself, traffic homicide investigation training is among the most intensive training the Florida Highway Patrol offers. There is an additional fourteen to sixteen weeks of training for certification into the program. The largest part of an investigation is comprised of advanced mathematical formulas, and the investigator must have a thorough knowledge of the laws of physics and conservation of energy."

Specifically, she said, "There are three levels of traffic homicide investigation; basic, advanced, and certified crash reconstructionist. In between those levels are specific courses for different types of vehicle crashes, such as motorcycle, commercial motor vehicle, pedestrian, and pedicyclist. In addition, there are required classes for scene measurement using a process called photogrammetry and laser measuring devices. It takes about two years to obtain the required certifications for the Traffic Homicide Investigation Division. There are also annual update and recertification classes that vary from one to two weeks."

Trish obtained the highest level of certification, which allowed her to become an instructor. She taught the photogrammetry class for the Florida Highway Patrol and basic crash investigation at the Florida State College Criminal Justice Center, where she was an adjunct professor for more than two years.

I asked Trish to explain the main purpose of the traffic homicide investigation unit. She explained, "Any time there is a traffic incident that involves a fatality or potential fatality, it's the job of the traffic homicide investigator to conduct a complete investigation and total reconstruction of the crash or incident. This process involves an investigation into the pre-crash information about all individuals involved. The purpose of this is to rule out potential medical, psychological, or criminal issues for the drivers and any possible mechanical issues with the involved vehicles that may have been contributing factors. Roadway conditions are also analyzed. Most all investigations included the collection of blood samples of all drivers involved in the crash. All of these things are done to determine the cause or causes of the crash, to bring closure to the victim's family, and to hold those responsible accountable."

Trish continued, "Extensive measurements and photos are taken for reconstruction purposes and evidence documentation. A homicide report is a detailed accounting of pre-crash, at-crash, and post-crash events. It's utilized by the department to assist families in understanding what happened to their family member and for criminal and civil court proceedings. Court preparation is extensive as the investigator must be able to intelligently speak to how and why they came to the conclusions that they did. It's difficult because of the advanced mathematics and physics that are used in the reconstruction of the crash. Being able to convey this process in lay terms has to be practiced, and investigators must be prepared to rigorously defend their investigation and the conclusions they reached. Defense attorneys and insurance companies will always bring in their own experts to counter an investigator's findings."

As a traffic homicide investigator, Trish would work the same shift as regular patrol units, days and evenings, but was on call three to four nights a week. On call was rotated among the investigators in her unit. Due to their caseloads and frequent court appearances, they didn't work midnight shifts. However, the on-call investigator would get called to work any fatality, regardless of the time of day.

Her career-defining moment came from a tragic event, a traffic fatality involving a child. She explained, "Early on in my career, I learned to despise drunk drivers. While this particular crash was not my investigation, I was a witness to a driver's statement that left me speechless. It occurred on Interstate 95 in downtown Jacksonville, Florida. A small toddler had been left unrestrained in a van. The child managed to unlock the rear doors of the van as it was in motion. The child fell from the van as it was travelling nearly fifty miles per hour and was immediately struck by a semi-tractor trailer. Not to be graphic, but there was nothing recognizable about the child.

"As the traffic homicide investigator approached the mother, who was the driver of the van, he attempted to be as sympathetic as possible considering what had just happened. It was grossly evident that the mother was very drunk. When the investigator asked her if she could tell us what happened, this was her response: 'Is this going to take long? I have a date tonight.' How much alcohol can one have in her system to respond like that? Her child had just been violently killed, and all this mother could think about was her date later that evening. From that point on, I never had one moment of sympathy for a drunk driver."

Trish described the most difficult part of her job. "There were many aspects of the job that took a toll. It's heartbreaking to knock on a door at three a.m. to tell a family their loved one was not coming home. There was never an easy way to do this, and I can remember every person I had to tell this news to. I remember their looks of disbelief and their cries of anguish as well as their anger, often times directed toward me.

"Traffic homicide is a gruesome investigation. Very seldom do individuals die unmutilated or left how their family remembers them. Having to see and smell this carnage, scene after scene, burns into the brain to the point that it has never left me. I make a conscientious effort to not think about the cases I handled. I know what can happen on a roadway in a split second, so I don't ever comfortably ride in a vehicle, and I am never at ease when loved ones are travelling until they are safely at their final destinations."

The most rewarding part of the job for Trish was this: "Bringing closure to families. If a loved one was killed at the hands of an impaired driver, bringing that driver to justice for the victim's family always gave me satisfaction. A dangerous person was taken off the highway and would not be out there to destroy another family. Also, I enjoyed being able to thoroughly investigate crashes so I could assure drivers that there was nothing they could have done differently to prevent the crash. Many times, drivers who are completely faultless in a crash feel responsible and second-guess their actions thinking if they had just done something different. By conducting the investigations the way I did, I felt as if I was providing peace of mind for them."

The Reciprocation of Respect

I asked Trish if there was anything she would like to say to people outside of the first responder world, and she replied: "I know how frightening it can be to encounter a police officer. I tried to always be aware of this when dealing with the public. Please allow officers the opportunity to do their job before you pass judgement on them. We hurt, we cry, and we get angry; you just aren't allowed to see it while we're doing our job. So, try to imagine what the end of our day looks like after having to hold in all these emotions. We age well beyond our actual years, and sadly for many, retirement is cut short by stress-related medical issues. If you treat an officer with respect, you will often find that respect returned."

Trish is married and retired now and is embracing her life after law enforcement. She still loves the outdoors and spends time playing golf, kayaking, travelling the world, photographing the wonders of mother nature, and as a Florida State Golf Association volunteer, working golf events.

Thank you, Trish, for your service to your community! Keep enjoying your Phase 2 retirement life; you earned it!

K9 Sergeant David Bell

Tallahassee Police Department
Retired: Twenty-Nine Years of Service

I've known David for many years. Even though we worked for the same department, we never had the opportunity to work together. At the time, though, our department believed in and supported the Florida Police Olympics, and David and I played on the coed softball team. We were actually pretty good, winning the gold medal several years.

It was a great time to get to know folks better away from the job and to meet officers and their families from all over Florida. As time went on, we all started having kids, tore tendons and ligaments, broke bones, and simply just got older. We tucked away our competitive urges and quietly retired from competition. David and I remained friends, and I attended his wedding to fellow teammate and forensic technician, Adrienne.

Growing up, David always knew that he wanted to do a fun and athletic job. For him, firefighter or police officer seemed to be the most likely choices. College was in the plans first, and he began his coursework at Florida State University in the College of Criminology. In order to earn his degree, he had to complete an internship. For this purpose, he chose the Tallahassee Police Department (TPD).

Not the Rookie Please

That choice forever changed David's life. He told me this story: "When I was an intern in July 1988, I was assigned to the patrol division for a week. I was placed with a dayshift squad. I remember sitting in the back of the check on room, which is where officers gather prior to the beginning of their shifts for updates, important information, and such. I watched as all the veteran officers arrived. When they saw me, an intern, they immediately hid. They didn't want to be chosen as the one I would ride with. No one wanted an intern.

"I remember seeing a young officer arrive in check on. I prayed he would take me or that the sergeant would put me with him. It didn't work out that way. I was put with a veteran officer who had me until another officer arrived at work in an hour or so. As we drove, I heard this veteran officer cuss, speed up, and then erupt into an unbelievable amount of emotion.

"He then yelled that an officer had been shot. We drove toward the scene at unbelievable speeds. It seemed as though every vehicle was driving slowly in front of us and not moving over. Upon arrival, we pulled into the scene. I could see the shot officer lying on the ground. The second officer [the young one I wished I could have ridden with] came over and gave us as much of a description as possible.

"We pulled into a neighborhood and began driving, looking for the suspects. The veteran officer told me to look on my side of the street. I recall seeing a female standing next to the road up ahead of us. We stopped, and I asked if she had seen anyone run. She said she was the one who called 911. The veteran officer asked, 'Called about what?'"

"The two guys covered in blood," she said.

"Where are they," he asked?

"In that house." She pointed at the next house up, on the driver's side of our patrol car.

The veteran officer told me to get down on the floorboard or run. I chose to run and get help. "Now here I am, a college intern with no police knowledge and no weapon. I don't know anything. The scene unfolds right in front of me. The suspects are located and dropped on the ground in front of me. Some tactical officer who had carried one suspect on his shoulders drops him right in front of me and tells me to watch him as he goes back to get the second suspect.

"Again, I know nothing, but here I am at ground zero. Some suspect had shot and killed an officer, an officer I was just in check on with about thirty minutes ago. I'm staring at bullet wounds, blood, and seeing an unbelievable amount of emotion from arriving officers.

The suspect started rambling. I didn't know what to say, so I said nothing.

"The following days, other officers made sure to contact me. They offered to let me ride with them on patrol. They wanted to make sure I was okay. Their concern and the citizens' positive and comforting remarks to those officers I rode with, made me realize I was staying here and policing this community. And I'm glad I did.

"Fifteen years later, I walked up to the veteran officer I rode with that day and asked if he knew who I was. He gave me a weird look, and we talked a little, but no talk about that day. I finally told him who I was. He lost his mind. He said he had talked about that intern to people and said that kid probably is in a mental institution or something. He saw a lot of stuff that day.

"We laughed. I might need some mental help, but that day and the following days solidified my career choice."

I remember this day well. It was July 8, 1988. I was a field training sergeant, and we had a pretty new group of rookies that the squad was training. We had worked that zone just ten hours earlier. The officer killed in the line of duty that morning was Officer Ernest Kerns Ponce de Leon. He was survived by a son and a daughter.

Moving through the Ranks

David completed his internship and graduated from FSU later that year. He was hired by TPD as an officer. He completed the police academy and the Field Training Officer program and began his career as a patrol officer.

For the next eighteen years, David had several different assignments, which included the Problem Oriented Policing Squad (POP) that targeted specific areas in the community experiencing particular problems. These could range from street-level drug sales to a neighborhood having an increase in auto burglaries. He also served as a Drug Abuse Resistance Education (DARE) officer working in Tallahassee's elementary schools, was a field training officer, a burglary investigator, and was assigned to the Vice and Narcotics Unit as a tech officer.

In addition, David became a hostage negotiator in 1991, and in 1993, he was chosen as a sniper for the Tactical Apprehension and Control Team (TAC). TAC was the name for the department's SWAT team.

K9 Handler

In 1999, he became the Vice Unit K9 handler, working Rusty, a single-purpose drug dog. As David said, "That means Rusty only did one thing, and that was search for narcotics."

In 2006, David was assigned to the department's Internal Affairs Unit as an investigator. His promotion to sergeant followed in 2007, and he returned to the patrol division. In 2010, David was chosen as the sergeant overseeing the department's K9 Unit, which consisted of seven K9 teams. He retired from this position in 2018.

Many people don't realize the training time and expense it takes to have effective K9 teams, so I asked David to elaborate on this. "Our department followed the Florida Department of Law Enforcement (FDLE) training model for K9 Units. To start, each K9 handler and K9 went through four hundred hours of documented training.

"Some of it was for the handler specifically and included state law and our department's policies and procedures. Obviously, the training also included learning how to handle your K9 partner. We bought our K9s from dealers, and we bought K9s called 'green' K9s. This meant they had no formal training but knew how to bite correctly. They bit and held.

"We then used our own trainers at TPD to train the handler and the K9. The hours are now up to four hundred eighty for the K9 teams. That usually worked out to four or five months of training before they were ready to try and certify with FDLE.

"If they passed certification, they were allowed to work the streets. We had to certify once a year with FDLE, and because our department cared and had the resources, we also chose a nationally recognized K9 certification. We separated the two certifications so that we completed one every six months or so. This made our K9 teams always ready, and it was pretty daunting for a defense attorney to prove that our K9s were not reliable in court.

"Only the vice dog was a single-purpose K9. They were only trained to search for specific illicit narcotics. All of our patrol dogs were dual-certified; they were trained in one of the two odors: illicit narcotics or explosives and patrol work.

"We had a bomb dog for a time, but the only calls for bombs were at or around the Capital Building, so we stopped training bomb dogs and let the Capital Police K9s handle them. When I retired, we still had one single-purpose drug dog in our Special Investigations Division, and seven dual-purpose patrol dogs.

"The illicit narcotics that we teach them to locate are cannabis, cocaine [powder and crack], methamphetamine, heroin, and MDMA. The patrol work included obedience, apprehension work, building and area searches, and tracking.

"The main purpose of a K9 unit was to support our patrol division and any special investigations. K9 patrolled the city and responded to calls for service that might require our assistance to officers. We trained a lot with at least sixteen hours each month for each K9 team. This showed that we were ready for any call and proved to the courts that we were reliable.

"I'll say this, the more you train, the better a K9 team you'll be. That's interesting to me how that shows up in our lives and jobs so much. Those who worked at their craft were generally the best at it.

"Different laws and current case law dictated when and how you could use our K9 partners. Our department followed the Graham vs. Connor case law. It used 'objective reasonableness.' Was the decision to use your K9 partner to apprehend or search for a suspect reasonable based on the information you, the handler, had at the time? Our decision took in the severity of the crime, danger to the officer or citizens, and the risk of flight by someone.

"Basically, you better be fast on your feet and quick with your thought process if you want to be a good K9 handler. You must understand when and why you can use your K9 partner on a call for service. If you don't, it might cost you your job.

"As an example, I may go to a high-priority call and ask officers if they need K9 help. I get information from them, and I make the decision to use or not to use my partner. Maybe I see a theft in progress, but if it's a misdemeanor, then I can't and will not use my K9 to chase and apprehend the suspect. The crime doesn't merit that amount of possible injury to catch this suspect. Will I pull my partner out of the vehicle and give loud verbal commands to the suspect that I'm going to let my K9 loose to find him? Yes. Will I? No.

"Our K9s were very much a deterrent to people fighting and running away from us. People were scared, and rightfully so, of our K9s. When I stood outside my vehicle with my K9 partner, and people saw him, they changed their thought process a lot and chose not to fight us or run from us because of the fear of being caught and bitten.

"People who were actively fighting the police and then saw and heard a police dog running at them stop because of the fear of being bitten.

"We had heat alarms on all of our trucks to hopefully keep our K9 partners from being injured or dying while in them. Especially in Florida, heat is our partner's enemy. Vehicle issues, engine stalls, and A/C stops have and would kill a dog. Our heat alarms were installed to cause our rear windows to drop and air the car out and alarm the handler.

"Ballistic vests for K9s in Florida were a tough call. Putting a vest on the K9 caused them to overheat even faster in our Florida heat. If we put it on him, he could have easily died trying to track or locate a suspect. Our K9s were so driven that they would continue to track a suspect while they were overheating and could end up dying while trying to locate the person. Drive was great, but the handler had to watch his partner and rely on his personal knowledge of him. We might have had to stop a track to avoid losing him."

I asked David about his favorite position at the police department, and he said it was a tie between the POP Squad and K9. As he said at the beginning of his career, he wanted a job that was fun and athletic. According to David, both of these positions "were exciting and physically challenging."

While they might have been his favorite, they were also the most difficult. David said, "You better be in great physical shape to do either of those jobs!"

This tied into what David felt was the best part of his job. "When you conducted a track with your K9 partner, and you located the suspect or missing person, that was priceless. It was like a kid hitting a homerun. All of our hard work and training paid off, and it was a great feeling."

But David had another experience as the K9 unit supervisor that was difficult, not just for him but for the entire unit. As he said, "Dealing with real life issues proved much harder than work issues.

The Loss of a Colleague and a Friend

"Prior to my arrival as the K9 Sergeant, Officer Kirk Watson, the K9 Unit lead team trainer, had been diagnosed with cancer. He had gone through treatment and was in remission. About a year after my arrival, Kirk informed me and our team of the return of his cancer. He kept me updated about his treatments and would let me know when he didn't feel as though he could work. But when he could work, he worked hard in spite of the monster that was inside him.

"The team wanted to help Kirk, but he was a strong, proud man. He didn't want us to feel sorry for him. He promised me often that he wasn't too sick to work and continued to work hard; he did everything he said he would do…except paperwork, he was terrible at turning in paperwork.

"He called in sick some days. Others, he just wasn't one-hundred percent, so I sent him to our K9 training area where he could catch up on paperwork and work on training matters for the unit. Kirk loved to work and loved the K9 unit. He often said his job gave him a sense of peace, so for me and knowing how important this was to Kirk, this was my way of keeping him working.

"Kirk was a great K9 trainer. He was incredibly knowledgeable, and the handlers listened to him. All of us knew how much he cared about us as handlers and friends. He was emphatic about knowing state law and case law and constantly stressed to do the right thing with our K9s, always. He was a very important piece of our team.

"While working and fighting cancer, Kirk had a terrible event occur. While he was on vacation, he left his K9 partner at the veterinary hospital that our department utilized. While in their care, his K9 partner suffered from bloat, which caused his stomach to swell up, and passed away. Kirk was obviously devastated at losing his K9 partner but now also worried about his position on our K9 team.

"New promotions and new bosses above me brought an uneasy feeling about whether Kirk would be allowed to stay on the team. After what seemed like an eternity, really two months, my bosses told me that I could decide on whether Kirk stayed. Kirk and I had a long talk about his health. He confirmed that he could do the work and really wanted to stay. He told me he had a retirement plan with a date, and the new K9 assigned to him would get him there. He and his new partner trained hard and became a great team.

"About eighteen months later, Kirk called me one day and said he was sick and at the hospital. He asked for me and the team to come visit him. He informed us that he was dying. Kirk left the hospital a few days later and passed quickly at his home surrounded by family and friends.

"I'm proud to say how well our department's command staff handled everything. They worked to get all of his retirement paperwork completed and never thought twice when I asked if his family could keep his K9 partner.

"We don't always lose our friends and coworkers to violence but sometimes to terrible diseases like cancer. We are human just like everyone else."

When asked about his own career-defining moment, David shared a moment that has stayed with him to this day. "I responded to a car crash that was close to our city/county line. When I arrived, it was horrific. You could see the amount of force involved in the crash by the extent of damage to both cars.

"Pieces of the cars were everywhere. It was determined that the crash occurred in the county outside of my [our department's] jurisdiction. Our sheriff's department was responding to the scene to handle the crash. Emergency Medical Services (EMS) personnel were already there.

"One person was deceased in her car. EMS was working on the extraction of other people in the car that was determined to be at fault. People had started to arrive at the crash scene.

"As it turned out, the single occupant, who was deceased, was the mother of some of these arriving people. She had missed the turn into the neighborhood, called and talked to them, turned around, and while she was on the way back to them, a car struck her head-on in her lane. The family had come out to greet their mother, heard the crash, heard the sirens, ran down to the scene, and saw their mom in the car.

"As we waited for the Sheriff's Office to arrive, the family was yelling at me to cover their mother up. Since the Sheriff's Office was primarily handling the scene, they had requested we leave it alone, and that included the mother. They didn't want us to alter the scene in any way but to wait on their arrival to work the crash. This was not uncommon for any scene, yet something the public doesn't understand.

"The crying and emotions were unbearable. It is one of the calls I have never forgotten. I still say a prayer for that woman I never met and the total senselessness of the crash. The raw feelings of that family that night was unforgettable."

David's wife was a crime scene forensic technician. But when they started a family, she left TPD and now works in the state crime lab at FDLE. Together they have two wonderful, active children.

David retired in 2018 and was able to retire his K9 partner, Luke, and bring him home with him.

David and K9s Buster, Rusty, and Luke, thank you for your service to your community. Enjoy retirement and your Phase 2 life!

Chief Bob Stewart

**Metro Washington D.C. Police Department: Twenty-Two Years
Tallahassee Police Department: One Year
Ormond Beach Police Department: Five Years
Retired: Twenty-Eight Years of Service**

I spend a good bit of time thinking about whom to highlight in my books. There are certain criteria I ponder. Bob was someone I wanted in the first *Behind and Beyond the Badge*, but he declined. I accepted his decision until I decided to write Volume II.

We met for lunch, and after catching up, I told him I was writing a second book. He asked questions, such as what the response was to Volume I, what I was attempting to accomplish with Volume II, and other related thoughts. For me, I always found our conversations fascinating as he holds unique perspectives. The timing seemed right, and I asked Bob again if he would consider letting me tell his story. A silent pause occurred, followed by a "let me think about it" response. A few weeks later, he emailed me with his approval.

Bob comes from a strong family unit. His father was a social worker who had been a first lieutenant during World War II. He introduced Bob to most of the ethnic centers in his hometown of Pittsburgh, Pennsylvania, because he wanted him to find something of value in each. He recognizes now that "This has been critical to my view of, and interaction with, the world around me."

His mother was a school teacher in the city school system. In his words, she "was made out of something extraordinary." He said, "My dad and I were hanging out at home on a Saturday afternoon. My mother left the house not sharing where she was going. She came back later and asked my dad if he would put the ladder in the car. He did as she asked but questioned why she needed it.

"She, in turn, asked us what we were doing, and our response was nothing. Mom told us to come with her and drove us to our church. She had grown so weary of the seeing dirt on the walls behind the pulpit that she had chosen to do something about it." His mother had cleaned as high as she could reach and needed the ladder to finish the job. Bob said, "I get my work ethic and sense of taking action genetically!"

Bob began his law enforcement career in the 1960s, a time of unrest in the United States with civil rights and the Vietnam War standing out as the headlines of the times. For Bob, "1968 and 1969 were terrible years. I was having horrible relationship issues, wasn't doing well in college, and it became clear that I wouldn't graduate on time. I wasn't in a good place and went to my draft board and asked if they would extend my draft deferment.

"They denied my request. I quit college and applied for a job with the Metropolitan Police Department (MPD) in Washington D.C." Bob was hired by MPD on May 26, 1969, the same date as his first draft notice. The draft board allowed him to complete the police academy before his induction into the United States Army in October. With regards to MPD, he said, "I was really looking for a temporary haven so that I could finish college but found a permanent home." Bob was in and out of the Army without ever leaving the States and came back to MPD.

However, "My entry into policing was not a popular one in my family or among my friends. There was a very thin line between the fear and trepidation that friends and family had when a loved one became a law enforcement officer and a social stigma that I have found fascinating. I think it was a mixture of the kind of historic resentment that most, if not all, minorities felt toward the police as oppressors. There's also a view among some middle-class minorities that policing is an unskilled labor or vocational job. It's not professional. Based on my mom and dad's reaction, this most certainly included them."

When Bob started with the MPD, he began where most new officers do, as a street patrol cop. His next assignment was with a plain clothes squad, which is where he says he has his "own version of the story about having almost shot a kid. A lot of cops have their own "*I-almost-shot-someone*" stories. I would have been justified. This kid pointed a fake gun at me that his older brother had been using for street robberies. Luckily, I didn't shoot him.

"About that same time, we had another officer shoot a kid in the back for stealing a planted bicycle. Rules and laws were different back then, and it was cleared as a justified shooting. That wouldn't happen today and shouldn't. This cop went on permanent desk duty but probably should have been retired. I can still see the perpetual, vacant look in that cop's eyes."

Bob went back to school and earned his bachelor of arts degree in political science from Howard University in 1974. "While in school, I took a number of political science, criminal justice, and public administration classes. Following the 1968 riots, police departments started hiring many more minorities and women, and it opened the gates to promotion and assignments that just didn't exist before.

"The years between 1968 and 1972 would be filled with a flood of research and writing about policing. The notion of Community Policing would be born; we would see landmark studies about policing and American Criminal Justice. The 911 system would be inaugurated, and it all came from the Challenge of Crime in a Free Society, a report by the President's Commission on Law Enforcement and Administration of Justice. I didn't notice the change because it was so subtle. I was not only in a law enforcement career; I had become a student of American policing. I remain one – after all of these years.

Frequent Promotions

"I became a field training officer, and I joined our Civil Disturbance Unit (CDU). I remained an active CDU member throughout my career. We had regular jobs within our districts but were called out for critical incidents around the city or on the Washington Mall where most demonstrations took place. We had additional semi-annual training. Not only did we augment our Special Operations Division for mass demonstrations, but we also provided initial response to critical incidents within our districts since we were authorized to carry shotguns."

Bob continued, "I had grown comfortable in my skin. I felt fully prepared and confident in my role as a patrol officer. I could tell my bosses were preparing me to be a supervisor. I had two very good lieutenants and an excellent captain. This captain would try to coax me into joining at least two of his units down the road, and he would eventually become the police chief after I retired.

"I went on to have a wonderful career at MPD. It's a big department, and I got transferred or promoted almost every two years. It would round out my career and resume very nicely as I had a great mix of operational and administrative jobs. As I look back on it, maybe the best result was to swap out partners every couple of years."

Law enforcement promotional processes vary, but many require written and oral exams. With that comes a mound of study material. In the 1970s, African Americans in the MPD had started to get promoted in greater numbers. This was due to highly structured study groups that had begun to form during the generation of black cops immediately senior to Bob.

When those cops began gathering regularly, it was viewed with suspicion by the department's all-white command staff. Bob said, "Internal Affairs sat outside and took photos and names of all those who participated. It was thought that they were meeting to plot some sort of insurrection. The bad old days were very bad."

In my interviews, I ask everyone to provide me with what he or she considers a career-defining moment. Bob's is somewhat different, but it's tied into those study groups. He explained, "I had attended a promotion ceremony, which for the MPD are "extravaganzas." They're typically held in one of the federal building auditoriums with lots of news coverage.

"After the ceremony, a newly promoted sergeant, who had been in one of my study classes, came up to me and asked if I would go with him to the other side of the auditorium. This sergeant had tried to get promoted twice before and had studied with a different group. He almost gave up since he had already sacrificed nearly two years with no return on his investment of time and energy.

"People who studied hard once but didn't get promoted typically didn't try again. This guy finally made it on his third try, and he performed well after getting promoted.

"When we reached the other side of the auditorium, he introduced me to his wife and two children, telling them, 'I just wanted you to meet Captain Stewart. I never would have been promoted if it wasn't for him.'

"There it was, the best day of my career! And by now, all of those early naysayers, including my parents, had changed their tune."

Bob did, in fact, rise through the ranks with assignments at all levels in the Field Operations Bureau. He also had assignments in Executive Protections and the Planning and Development Division. He retired from MPD in 1991 at the rank of captain, having served for twenty-two years.

In all of Bob's years in various assignments, he suffered many losses, similarly to anyone who has worked in law enforcement. "There was a time in my career where we would suffer horrific events. Several were line-of-duty deaths, including a female officer who was shot responding to a bank robbery (and the first female police officer killed in the line of duty in the U.S.), an officer who drowned trying to save a person attempting suicide, and one of our police helicopters crashed killing the pilot and an observer doing a ride-along in the helicopter. We also had a female sergeant, a friend of mine, killed off duty in a domestic incident. The deaths are not always in shootouts with bad guys. There are always more victims than meet the eye. Then there was the song *Amazing Grace* that was always played on the bagpipes at the funerals. I just can't do the bagpipes anymore."

A Never-Ending Career

However, Bob wasn't finished with his career in law enforcement after retirement. He applied for and was selected as a major with the Tallahassee Police Department (TPD). This is where I met Bob and where Bob met his wife, Cheryl. Cheryl had been one of the recruits trained by my field training squad. Like Bob, she had been in the Army but remained in the reserves, something Bob wishes he had done.

Bob said, "The Tallahassee Police Department was the best police organization I worked in. It's a well-educated, well-trained, well-equipped department. The pay scale is competitive, and the retirement isn't bad at all. There's a good moral compass. TPD has been accredited by the Commission on Accreditation for Law Enforcement Agencies (CALEA) longer than almost any other department in the country.

"Cheryl was one of the first people I met when I got to TPD. There was still a sense of 'family' that you don't often find in mid-size and big departments anymore.

"I got to Tallahassee in March of 1991. During my in-processing, I went to the personnel unit. Cheryl was on limited duty recovering from knee surgery. Remember, I was coming from Washington, D.C. where the Redskins play. I looked into Cheryl's cubicle where I was being introduced to her. She had a New York Giants pennant pinned up to the room divider. My exact words were, 'You and I will not be getting along at all.'"

Bob continues. "I was enjoying my time and my assignment at TPD. After a year, I realized I had not been in a competitive promotion or selection process since I applied to TPD. My plan was to merely test the waters and get into a chief's selection process for practice. I applied to St. Petersburg, Fort Lauderdale, and in what was a fluke, Ormond Beach. There was a flyer for the Ormond Beach job in the TPD breakroom, and it had been copied so many times that it was almost sideways when hung straight. Since my resume was already updated and ready to go, I thought, *Why not?*

Ormond Beach Police Department

"I was in the running for Ormond Beach and St. Petersburg and became a finalist in both. I heard nothing from Fort Lauderdale. When the city manager in Ormond Beach found out I was a frontrunner in St. Petersburg, my stock went way up. I was offered the chief's job in Ormond Beach, and it was time to move. This would be the first of a number of times that my relationship with Cheryl would be long distance, but not so far that we couldn't make it work.

Out of about one hundred sworn officers at the Ormond Beach Police Department, Bob and one other were the only African-Americans. As Bob stated, "We completely over-represented the entire minority population in Ormond Beach."

Bob's plan was to stay in Ormond Beach for three years, but he ended up staying for five. "There's not a personality or leadership template that fits all effective police bosses. The road is a lot easier for those who take over a well-oiled machine. You just have to be smart enough not to screw it up. If you come from inside the same department, the way forward should be smooth since you know everybody, and they know you. When you're the outsider, it's a horse of a different color. You don't know who to trust, and nobody trusts you.

"In only the largest departments are you going to be able to bring in your team with you. The key positions in the department have incumbents, some of whom have contractual guarantees that make it tough to move them around. It's important to get the right people in the right seats as quickly as you can. Typically, if you're from the outside, the city manager or mayor is expecting you to change some things. You'll need support and assistance from those who buy into your vision for the department's future.

"In my opinion, the one big mistake I see police bosses make is surrounding themselves with butt kissers and snitches. It may feel good to have all those people buttering up to you – telling you what a good boss you are – but it will kill your career faster than anything else. Only bad things come out of those scenarios.

"When I got to Ormond Beach, they were being sued by several current and former employees in reference to sexual harassment. The local chapter of the National Organization for Women had been carrying signs up and down the sidewalk outside of police headquarters. The department was also under investigation by the United Stated Department of Justice for the acts that were at the heart of the litigation.

"I was able to get the people I needed in the top two management positions. Both of these guys would go on to be police chiefs as would our Internal Affairs Sergeant. I'd like to think that I helped in some way. I'm very, very proud of this.

"Much of my first year was filled with working on new policies and training concerning sexual harassment issues that had created that environment directly and indirectly. The rest of the ride was mostly positive. We got a Police Athletic League started in the black neighborhood in town, and we organized a Citizen's Police Academy (CPA) before they got to be so popular, and a CPA Alumni Association that is still strong and very active."

As Bob was reaching his fifth year in Ormond Beach, he started to look for the next move in his journey. In 1997, Bob retired from law enforcement and became the executive director of the National Organization of Black Law Enforcement Executives (NOBLE), a position he held for three years.

He said, "I had been active in the National Organization of Black Law Enforcement Executives as a young sergeant in D.C. NOBLE was founded in 1976, and I joined in 1978, in time to attend my first conference in Baltimore. I became a life member while I was a lieutenant and held positions in the D.C. Metro

Chapter and on the National Board. It was a natural fit, and the timing was perfect for me to become the NOBLE Executive Director. I took office just as we moved racial profiling to the top of our national discussion. If there was a meeting or conference about racial profiling or bias-free policing, I got invited.

"I broadened my network of associates and acquaintances in the "professional" end of policing. The industry is supported by elements of the United States Department of Justice (USDOJ), police organizations, unions, and think tanks that include researchers, consultants, and other criminal justice practitioners. Most cops are unaware of the roles and functions of this complex network beyond the unions. This is eventually where I will spend the next years of my life's journey and remain today."

Race and Policing

"I know that a number of cops don't like the topic of race and policing. The discussions on racial profiling made us begin to address this issue, but we still seem to struggle with the mere mention of race and policing in the same sentence. A lot of this failure is due to us not talking enough about it. During the Vietnam War, the military started to address the issue of race head on, and now the military is the most integrated segment of our society. I've always felt that we could learn lessons from the military.

"In policing, we've begun to train on implicit bias, something that we all could use a dose of. I see two important results. I spend a lot of time talking about race and even more time listening to others attempt to have the conversation. What I hear is one person talking about racism, one talking about bigotry, another talking about stereotypes, and another talking about discrimination. They all think they're having the same conversation. Our knowledge and understanding of implicit bias make for a richer and more coherent and meaningful discussion about race.

"The second big benefit has been teaching police supervisors how to approach officers who they suspect may be knowingly or unknowingly profiling. They can then counsel them without calling them a racist and make them aware that there may be patterns to their stops, discretionary arrests, or vehicle searches that might be influenced by unconscious stereotypes and/or biases.

"When you think about it, with all of their experience and the view that we have about human behavior, maybe the police should be leading the discussion on race relations.

"As my third year at NOBLE drew to a close, it became pretty clear to me that I could have a fairly successful career as a consultant and that I would not go back to active police work. I had a three-year contract with NOBLE and chose not to renew it."

When looking back at his law enforcement career, Bob added, "Every police management book says that patrol is the backbone of the department. Typically, most people seem to be trying to get out of patrol and into a specialized unit. Very often these are referred to as 'elite' units by a completely ignorant press and news media. I'm incensed every time I hear or read it. Citizens are much more likely to interact with a member of the patrol force before anyone else in the agency. It's a patrol officer who gives us our biggest and best opportunity to impress a citizen with our knowledge, professionalism, and courtesy, and to give that citizen a favorable impression of our department."

In 2000, Bob created his consulting company, Bobcat Training, and has been working at that nonstop ever since. He is a federally recognized police practices expert and trainer throughout the United States and internationally. He's been an expert witness in a few noteworthy civil cases and continues to serve as a monitor in a number of consent decrees.

Bob and Cheryl married in 1999. Bob's law enforcement career was ending, but Cheryl's was on the rise. There was always something special about watching recruits rise through the ranks, and Cheryl did just that. She retired from TPD in 2013, as the Deputy Chief of Police, having served for twenty-six years. She also spent seven years active duty in the Army and another eighteen years in the reserves.

Bob added, "My wife, Cheryl, and I were probably both prewired for police work. Neither of us grew up wanting to be cops. Cheryl was drawn to law enforcement while serving in the Army. We both brought lifestyles, personalities, value systems, ideologies, and skill sets that fit very nicely into the framework of policing and its culture. While I continue to be a student of American policing and focus on needed reforms, Cheryl, having completed a noteworthy and distinguished career of her own, plays better golf than I do."

When asked if he had any additional thoughts to share, Bob offered, "For those still in law enforcement who want to sit in the big chair one day as a chief, don't be afraid to stand apart from your peers in the mainstream and start leading, today.

"Life's pretty good. I recommend retirement to everyone. I look around and see other police retirees I know, and they're also doing pretty well, especially other retired law enforcement couples. Cheryl and I are not as unique as you might think.

"We're pretty laid back. We travel a bit, split time between houses in Florida and western New York, and follow a lot of sports in person, at home on TV, or in sports bars on the road. There are always at least two or three Siberian Huskies in the house, and life's mellow.

"After a lifetime of having the stiff upper lip, I find myself much more reflective, sentimental, and emotional. I tear up at the drop of a hat. Everything from the puppy antics you people post on Facebook to poignant news scenes of cops doing good and heroic work can make me weepy.

"My favorite emotional responses, however, are reserved for walk-off home runs, buzzer beaters, hail Mary passes, a Triple Crown Winner, every American Olympic gold medal, a walk-on player who moves up to the scholarship, every military homecoming, a loss by the Cowboys or any Boston or New England Team, a first-time winner in NASCAR, the National Anthem, and flyovers by the Blue Angels or Thunderbirds.

"As we drift away from the agencies we used to work for, we still "Back the Blue" in a number of ways. We support favored law enforcement funds and causes, thank officers who are currently serving for their efforts, and occasionally pay for their breakfast or lunch if we're in the same restaurant.

"I'll work for another five years or so, then put more work into my golf game. I need to get better before I'm done. Until then, a lot of my time will be spent with departments that are working to improve the state of American policing. My efforts will be largely focused on the training of future police leaders. I'll also spend considerable time urging promising young people, especially those who look like me, to consider policing as a career, even if their friends and relatives are urging them not to.

"Be safe, and we'll see you down the road!"

Thank you, Bob and Cheryl, for your service to your country and to your communities.

Commander Susan Jeter

Brevard County Sheriff's Office
Retired: Twenty-Eight Years of Service

I have known Susan for more than fifty years. Not only did we grow up in the same small town of Titusville, Florida, but we lived across the street from each other and were high school classmates. After high school, we both moved to Tallahassee, Florida, to attend college. Unsure of her professional path, Susan left school and enlisted in the United States Army in 1982.

She was trained as a combat medic and a Combat Warfare Specialist and stationed at Fort Riley in Kansas. Susan left the Army after three years as a sergeant but remained with the Army National Guard for an additional three years.

A career in law enforcement was not something either of us had talked about or considered, so I asked Susan why she chose this profession. She stated, "Honestly, when I left the Army and returned home, I needed a job. This is tough to admit, but I struggled. I lived out of my car for the first six months. I was working and trying to get back into college. I heard that the Brevard County Sheriff's Office (BSCO) was hiring, so I applied. Fortunately, I was invited for an interview with the jail commander, who was also a career Army guy; he was impressive.

"I was hired in November 1986, completed the academy in February 1987, and was sworn in as a corrections deputy sheriff. I thought I would stay for about a year and then try to get employment in the medical field. Obviously, I fell in love with the job and ended up staying twenty-eight years."

Susan was assigned to work in the Brevard County Jail as a corrections officer, became a field training officer, and was promoted to sergeant. She worked all shifts and was then promoted to lieutenant, serving primarily as the administrative lieutenant but filling in for regular shifts when needed. She was also involved with other aspects of the sheriff's department as a firearms instructor, human-diversity instructor, and as a member of the Crisis Intervention Team and the agency's honor guard. Susan was part of the Corrections Response Team as well. This involved serious training to prepare for escapes, riots, high-risk prisoner transports, and hostage situations that could take place at the jail, courthouse, or during a prisoner transport.

SWAT Team Medic

One of the things Susan enjoyed most was being a SWAT Team medic. She explained, "I loved being on the SWAT team. Training was intense, and for good reason. Situations that SWAT was called for could take several hours, and it required a new level of physical fitness for me. I went to SWAT Tactical Medic School and SWAT Medic EMT Certification School. These training classes were conducted by the United States Army Uniformed Services, University of Health Sciences, and the United States Park Police. With my Army background as a medic and these training classes, I earned a spot on our SWAT team and was part of the entry team. Like any member of a SWAT team, I was on call twenty-four hours a day, seven days a week."

Every first responder can recall at least one career-defining moment, and Susan is no different. It involved a SWAT call out to serve a high-risk, no-knock search warrant. It took place on Christmas Eve.

"As we entered the residence, I immediately saw a little boy, about five years old. Our entry had awakened him. He had been sleeping underneath his Christmas tree. As you can imagine, we were all dressed in full gear with helmets and weapons. He looked at us with such innocence and asked if we were Santa. There were no presents under the tree, and the house had no electricity. The residents were using car batteries for the lights on the Christmas tree. No ornaments were on the tree, just the lights. I stayed with that little boy and tried to explain that we were there to check on his daddy. Sadly, his mother and father were not home; he had been left alone. We were able to locate a relative to come and get him. This was one moment I will never forget; it changed me."

I asked Susan how this event changed her. "Even the criminals in society have families, and the hardest part is the effect it has on their children. They are so innocent, especially at that age. It truly opened my eyes and made me think. There are certainly some hardcore evil people in this world who need to be locked away for life. Some commit crimes to put food on their tables, and some otherwise good people just make poor decisions. No matter the circumstance, it's always the kids who are affected most."

First Female Jail Commander

While working, Susan completed her bachelor of science degree in 2004 and her master's degree in professional administration, with honors, in 2005. After serving as a major for one year and twenty total years with the agency, Susan was promoted that year to jail commander, where she remained for her final eight years with the Brevard County Sheriff's Office.

She told me her final position was quite an achievement. "I was the first woman in the state of Florida to serve as a jail administrator/commander. I was responsible for five hundred and thirty sworn and non-sworn personnel and a forty-one-million-dollar budget. At that time, we were the sixth largest jail in the state of Florida with an inmate population that often topped two thousand."

With her promotion and new responsibilities came the task of making improvements. "Our jail was extremely overcrowded and understaffed. Attempted suicides by inmates were at record numbers. Our newly elected sheriff and I undertook a jail expansion, which included a medical and mental health wing and a hiring plan to increase our staffing levels. We doubled the size of the jail and were able to nearly double our staffing. Our suicides and attempted suicides decreased each year, and we became the first jail in the state to train our corrections officers in crisis intervention."

Susan helped create change in other areas. "We worked to replace old equipment, such as computers, guns, vests, Tasers, and an antiquated inmate tracking system. We also started to use basic inmate labor on the construction projects, which saved over one hundred thousand dollars. With the help of the project manager, they created a training program that allowed qualified inmates to be certified as construction technicians.

"We started other programs where inmates could cook their own food, sew uniforms and bed sheets, and work in the laundry area. Inmates sorted recyclables at the landfill and used the profits to refurbish bicycles for underprivileged children. They grew plants suitable for landscaping county buildings and did the installation and maintenance of the landscaping. One of our most popular programs was Paws and Stripes, where inmates learned to train shelter dogs in basic obedience during an eight-week period. These dogs were then sent back to the shelter and available for adoption. If they had the desire, the inmates could receive certification as a dog handler and learn animal first aid."

Some of these programs were new and innovative at the time, especially the sewing program. It involved training willing inmates on industrial quality machines. Susan said, "The inmates would cut the heavy material used for the jail uniforms, then sew stacks of shirts and pants. Switching to this program instead of buying the uniforms was another cost-saving measure."

The Impact of Natural Disasters

I asked Susan what impact natural disasters, such as hurricanes, had on a jail facility. She said, "We worked until the threat of the hurricane had passed, which meant we would be at the jail for days. We were away from our families, who had to deal with whatever happened without us. That was always difficult. In Florida, we certainly know the impact hurricanes and other disasters can have and were more than willing to send people to Mississippi to help out after Hurricane Katrina made landfall."

We talked about the most rewarding part of her job and what she felt was the most difficult. The most rewarding aspect was easy for her to answer. "Watching the officers grow, get promoted, and garner recognition for their efforts. While I was commander, we had six officers awarded Corrections Officer of the Year by the Florida Sheriff's Association. It made me proud."

The most difficult part of her job was tougher to talk about, not uncommon for first responders. She mentioned the incident with the little boy on Christmas Eve but told me about a very tough situation. "It involved an officer's family member who committed suicide. There is so much stress associated with being a police officer or any first responder, but sometimes we forget the stress it creates for family members."

Susan wanted to pass these thoughts onto those outside the first responder profession. "When you hear something about someone in law enforcement, remember that there are always two sides to a story. Oftentimes the media will only portray the one who creates a story, a headline. When the other side of that story comes out, it often becomes a much smaller headline and is hidden on the back pages. Being a police officer or any first responder is a tough job, but we are just like everyone else. We have families and deal with all of the same issues, both good and bad."

Susan is very close with her family, and they were always supportive of her career. She was appointed by the Governor of Florida to serve on the Criminal Justice Standards and Training Commission but was only able to serve one year. Her mother was diagnosed with stage-four cancer, so she resigned her position and took time off to take care of her. Her sister was involved in a horrific traffic crash not long after, and Susan has since become her legal guardian.

New Life of a Real Estate Agent

When Susan retired in 2015, she moved to north Georgia and is now a real estate agent. Hiking and the outdoors have always been a love of hers, and one of her goals is to hike the entire Appalachian Trail. "I always like to challenge myself physically and mentally, and hiking is one way for me to do that. I am hiking the trail in sections, and I've completed two and a half states. This year I will be hiking all of New Hampshire and Maine, and if I accomplish that, it will be for a total of six hundred sixty-one miles. I like hiking the trail because it's a definite path with interesting landscape and a lot of history. I've met some great people on the hikes. Everyone is friendly and there to help each other."

Another feat she accomplished was the Cross Florida Ride. It's a one-hundred-seventy-mile bike ride from the east coast to the west coast. Susan also dabbles in photography and on occasion paints. She is enjoying her retirement and Phase 2 of her life.

Thank you, Susan, for your service to your country and to your community.

Andrew McClenahan

**Tallahassee Police Department:
Five Years Active Duty;
Five Years Reserve Officer
Florida Department of Environmental
Protection/Florida Fish and Wildlife Commission:
Ten Years
Active Duty: Fifteen Years of Service
Currently: Florida Department of Children and
Families, Director, Office of Public Benefits
Integrity: Five Years**

I've known Andy for more than twenty years, and when I approached him about letting me tell his story in this book he was hesitant. He didn't believe his story or his thoughts were anything special to write about... a response I often get from folks.

    I convinced Andy to meet me for coffee one morning to talk more about his story. He had read my first book and knew the premise and purpose of it but still wasn't convinced he was a fit for volume two. I asked him a few questions, then sat back and listened.

He got emotional at times, as did I, but we continued our chat. An hour and a half later, he agreed to let me tell his story. I believe Andy is an honest, hard-working man who speaks from the heart.

Andy is another example of someone who had no early thoughts of becoming a police officer. While in high school, he recalled taking a skills-career assessment test, and he told me the results. "The recommendations listed included: police officer, teacher, pastor, computer programmer, farmer, and circus employee. When I saw those, I thought, *I don't want to do any of those!* In hindsight, I've probably utilized all those skills at some point in my law enforcement career, except maybe farmer, although I think I have the work ethic of a farmer."

After high school, Andy attended Southern Illinois University as an accounting major. His intention was to become a Certified Public Accountant, go to law school, and practice corporate law. None of that happened.

He left Southern Illinois University and moved to Tallahassee, Florida, to live with his parents and enrolled at Florida State University. As Andy described, "Being a transfer student meant my grade point average came with me. I was constantly chasing the entrance requirement to be accepted into the accounting program despite having enough credit hours to declare accounting as a minor. I eventually had to declare a major, so I did some research. FSU had the nation's top criminology program, so I declared that as my major and thought I would focus on getting my law degree."

As with many college majors, Andy was required to complete a semester-long internship. A fraternity brother of his was completing his internship at the Leon County Sheriff's Office

(LCSO), so Andy applied and was accepted. At the completion of the internship, Andy was offered a job. "I had to start my employment with LCSO working at the jail. After a couple of years, I would have the opportunity to become a fully sworn road (patrol) deputy making eighteen thousand dollars a year. I left the internship with positive memories and experiences but with the mindset that being a cop wasn't for me."

Andy still had his sights set on attending law school, but an unexpected experience changed his mind. "Just before I graduated in the spring of 1991, I was summoned for jury duty for a two-week-long federal drug-smuggling case. As a full-time student, I had the option of being excused from serving; however, it seemed like a great opportunity to see what it was like to be a trial attorney. When it was over, I wanted nothing to do with being an attorney. I was definitely 'too smart to be an attorney!'"

Loss Prevention

After graduating from FSU with his bachelor of science degree in criminology, Andy decided he was done with school. He wasn't sure what to do career-wise but took a leap into corporate loss prevention with a large retail chain establishment. Andy admits he wasn't that good at catching shoplifters but said, "I was near the top of the corporate ranks in catching dishonest employees."

While working one day, Andy had this experience: "I got into a foot pursuit chasing a shoplifter who happened to be six-foot-four and looked as if he lifted weights every day. He left the store without paying for a two hundred ninety-nine-dollar jacket, a felony at the time. I had an epiphany of sorts. I was working horrible hours, fighting and detaining shoplifters, felons, armed only with a pair of handcuffs and a store security badge, for six dollars an hour. This wasn't for me or worth it."

Not long after that, Andy left corporate loss prevention and applied for the police academy. He became President of Recruit Class #130 at the Pat Thomas Law Enforcement Academy and graduated in May 1994. Florida had newly instituted a state certification examination, and no departments were hiring until the test was passed. Andy did pass and was recruited by agencies throughout Florida.

However, he had met his future wife, and they wanted to stay in Tallahassee, so he applied for employment with the Tallahassee Police Department. "The hiring process was a lengthy one, but each week I would either call TPD to check on the status of my application or show up in person in my only suit. I was hired in November 1994 and sworn in on January 9, 1995."

Patrol Officer

Andy spent five years with TPD working the streets as a patrol officer, a member of the Community Oriented Policing Squad, and as a field training officer. He described his patrol time. "I loved the pace of being a patrol officer. I was assigned to the same area of town for most of my time with TPD. It was a lower-income area with public housing complexes, sadly riddled with those who attempted to run street-level narcotic enterprises and prostitution. I took my job seriously and loved the positive interactions with the community, especially the kids. I wanted to do my part to help provide these kids and the other law-abiding citizens with a safe place to live and work. They knew me, and I knew them."

I pushed Andy to tell me what his most rewarding job at TPD was, and he said, "Nothing was more rewarding, personally and professionally, than being a field training Officer. I was blessed to have some great recruits that today span the rank structure at TPD up to Major. There are few things more rewarding than to hear someone proudly say that they were trained by you."

When I asked Andy why he left the Tallahassee Police Department, he spoke from the heart. It's a hard reminder of the effects the job can have on your personal life. "I never intended on leaving TPD; the men and women there are still like family to me. In hindsight, leaving TPD was the worst financial (retirement-wise) decision I ever made. Personally, it was the best and only one I could make.

Marriage and the Job

"In September 1996, I married Tricia. I still refer to her as my bride and do my best to date her and make her laugh every day. Unlike many cops, I refused to be the guy who referred to her as "my first wife" or "my current wife." I promised her I would dig ditches before I became another divorced cop statistic. Immediately after we were married, we moved into our first home. Despite living like two ships passing in the night because of my shift, I felt like we were making it work.

"I honestly believed I was making the most of my off-duty time with my bride. I didn't have cop posters on the walls or gun belts hanging from the bed. I really tried to 'protect' our marriage. I had a closet in a room on the opposite side of the house from our bedroom where all my gear would hang. It wasn't until I removed my sweat-soaked undershirt and vest, hung my uniform, and emerged from the room that 'Andy the Husband' was home.

"Yet the damage to our marriage was occurring despite my vigilant watch, something I wouldn't discover until years later. Working the midnight and afternoon shifts while she had a normal working schedule took its toll on us like the proverbial frog boiling in a pot.

"In September 1999, we gave birth to our son, Ryan. It was perhaps the greatest thing to ever happen to me. I will never forget that moment the nurse midwife called me over as the head emerged, 'Andy, get over here!' My first thought was, *Oh no. Something is terribly wrong.* Turns out she just wanted me to be the one who brought our child into the world. I delivered Ryan and proudly announced, 'It's a boy!' My purpose and meaning in life, in that instant, changed, forever."

Andy was a proactive street officer and a self-described workaholic. He knew his patrol area well including the problem areas. It was one of Tallahassee's busiest patrol zones. Andy added, "I saw the worst in people, just how depraved humanity can be and how broken the world was. I fought for my life wrestling people with guns. I almost shot a fourteen-year-old kid, I was shot at, and a street-level drug dealer even put a contract out on me. I left a lot of sweat, some blood, and a few tears on the street. But I kept all of that, all the crap, from my bride. I never brought those things home. I would share funny stories with her but never the bad stuff."

Once Ryan was born, Andy asked his sergeant how much time he could take off to be with his wife and son. This sergeant suggested he take a month off as it was time he would never get back, so Andy did. He told me, "Spending that time with Tricia and our son was precious, but I knew the time would come when I had to go back to work. That day did come, and it took me three tries to leave the house. I kept coming back to kiss them both. The realization that it could be the last time was never anything I thought about before that day."

Every shift after roll call, Andy would head to his patrol zone and to the main problem area to let those in the community know he was there; he was on-duty. Before his paternity leave, he felt that he was beginning to make a difference in that community. No more open drug sales or prostitution; it was changing for the better.

On his first day back to work, Andy drove to his zone. For him, it was as if he had never been there. Andy said, "I was dejected and perhaps a little naïve that I thought I had made a difference in the community and in someone's life. I questioned why I was putting my life on the line every day when in the big picture, it really didn't matter. Not only did I have a wife, but I now had a son; they were my world. I realized later that I did make a difference, but at that moment, it was hard to see."

Technology and the Job

Andy also had a penchant for working with computers and had become TPD's lead Mobile Data Computer instructor as they transitioned to having laptops in all patrol vehicles. Not long after his son was born, he had a conversation with another TPD officer. She had just completed her education in computer programming and was leaving the police department to enter the technology field. Andy decided that was a path for him as well.

Going back to school while working full-time and having a family was not easy, and he shared this. "I began balancing full-time computer programming schooling with afternoon shift work. I would drive my take-home patrol car to school at eight thirty in the morning and was in class until two in the afternoon. After class I would drive to the police station to work out, shower, and get ready for my work day to start at four p.m. We worked ten-hour shifts, and I always hoped to go home on time at two a.m. I'd get a few hours of sleep and do it again the next day. Not much time to be a husband or a father to our infant son. It was time I would never get back, and the frog continued to boil in the pot."

In 2000, Andy's wife Tricia was approached by an IT supervisor where she worked, inquiring how her husband was progressing in school. He wanted to meet with him about a possible job offer. Andy met with him and accepted the job offer, but remained a reserve officer at TPD for another five years.

Making this career change wasn't easy. "Making the adjustment from patrol shift work to a 'normal work life' was significantly harder than I could have imagined. I suddenly went from barely seeing my wife to seeing her all the time. We slept in the bed at the same time, fought for hot-water shower time, drove to work together, worked in the same building, on the same floor... just four offices away from each other.

In 2003, Andy was approached by a former TPD lieutenant who was working for the state of Florida. He was a major in charge of internal investigations with the Department of Environmental Protection, Office of Inspector General. He offered Andy a job as a captain, and he jumped at the opportunity to be a sworn officer again.

Andy added, "Despite my vigilance to watch for signs impacting my marriage, I became aware that we were in trouble. I was an insomniac, dealing with PTSD, like every single officer does, and had absolutely no idea of what Tricia had been going through alone. You see, cops aren't the only ones serving; the spouse does as well. I think the years of us having a part-time marriage had impacted her, and while I was physically present with her, I was still absent. I had no idea how much she needed me to be a contributing spouse at home and with our son. I sucked at it, and even though I'm not much better at it now, I at least try.

"For the next four years, I worked at saving my marriage, and at the same time, I emotionally attempted to rejoin the human race. When I think about it, 'saving' may be the wrong word. I don't think we were ever truly heading for a split, but the danger of it was certainly present as we worked on it. It wasn't a 'bad marriage,' but it had to get better, and it did.

Making Christ the Center

"In 2007, we found our new church home, and everything came together. Christ had truly become the center of our marriage.

My family was now intact. I think we face the same trials and tribulations as every other married couple, but we face it together with a solid foundation. I am painfully aware of my utter brokenness, but my hope and trust is rightfully placed in God. My identity is no longer in my job, so the successes and failures no longer impact me so completely in my head or heart."

Trying to balance shift work and family had an immense effect on Andy's life, and I asked him if there was a certain part of the job that was more difficult than another. He said, "The most difficult time for me was while working as a captain conducting internal affairs investigations with the Department of Environmental Protection and Florida Fish and Wildlife. I'm a firm believer in accountability, both in my personal life and my professional work. Nothing makes me angrier than someone tarnishing the badge and doing something intentionally wrong.

Take Responsibility

"Those people, and that's what they are, fallible humans who make mistakes and poor judgments, have no business being in the job. But there's a big difference between a good cop making a mistake or a poor decision and a cop who intentionally makes a wrong choice. If you make a mistake, just own it. If you're a good cop, your administration is typically going to support you. But don't lie about your actions. I lost a lot of respect for some of my brothers and sisters in uniform because they couldn't accept personal responsibility or accountability for a mistake. Take your lump and move on. Don't let that moment define your career.

"I never understood how someone could get from being a dedicated public servant to intentionally lying under oath about something that, in the grand scheme of things, wasn't a big deal. I was fortunate that I had a good reputation with the cops I had to interview. I let the chips fall where they may; I had no agenda or opinion either way. Still, that was the most difficult job I've ever had and one that unfortunately isn't held in high esteem by most cops."

When I asked Andy to talk to me about his career-defining moment, he couldn't offer just one. There were several situations that stood out and had a huge impact on him personally and professionally. I thought about each one and felt strongly that three should be included but for different reasons.

The first scenario occurred when Andy was in the early stages of his training as a new officer. He said, "I believe it was my sixth day on the job that altered my whole perception of what it meant to wear the uniform and badge. I was a rookie on midnight shift learning the streets when I responded to a local golf course pro shop for a burglary in progress. When we arrived, my training officer told me to cover the back door while he covered the other exit. As backup officers arrived that freezing cold night in January, the door I was covering from behind the starter shed opened, and out came the suspect. He was about fourteen years old and holding a full-sized revolver. Another officer, a member of our hostage negotiation team, began talking with him. He ignored my demands for him to drop his gun.

"Another responding officer shined his flashlight on the kid, backlighting (silhouetting) me. The kid began to raise his pistol to point at me while saying, 'I see one of you right there!' I had a perfect sight picture on him and began to pull the trigger. For some reason, one I can't explain today, something told me he wasn't going to shoot. I ducked my head back around the starter shed. After a long standoff, we were able to subdue the kid with less-lethal SAGE rounds – rubber mallet bullets.

"When I got home that night, I unholstered my duty weapon to put it away. I put the safety on and saw the hammer fall. It was in the 'half-cocked' position. I had been pulling the trigger to shoot and kill this kid in self-defense. The hammer had stopped halfway – and just a fraction more pressure would have cycled the round, firing the gun. It was at that moment that the true gravity of the responsibility imparted upon me hit me. I was given authority to take away the two most precious things to mankind – the power to arrest someone and take away their freedom and the authority to take a life when justified."

Losing My Guardian Angel

The second situation for Andy occurred shortly after he left the police department and was more personal. "Just weeks after I left TPD full-time, I got a phone call at home. It was the TPD dispatch center letting me know that a dispatcher, Tawana Scott, had perished in an automobile accident. This person wasn't just a dispatcher, she was the best one. But she was more than that calm, reassuring voice on the radio; she was my guardian angel on many nights.

"She was also my grounding rod for racial issues or questions. If there was something I didn't understand, from African-American slang, feelings about law enforcement, or a person to vent to, she was there for me. We had a special bond, my soul sister. I made sure to go say hi to her every week in the communications center. She was an incredible woman, a single mother with a high-school education. Her son was her world, and she worked hard to provide for him.

"She pulled double shifts and had begun looking for ways to invest her money, something she often asked advice about. I will never forget the day she called me to meet her at the police station. We walked out to the parking lot, and she showed me her brand-new car. That car was one of the financial goals we talked about.

"She died driving that car home after working a double shift. It was a head-on collision, and she died instantly. I had the hardest time at her funeral, and I still miss her to this day. She's probably a big reason why I never became a jaded cop, especially since I worked as a white male in a predominantly black community. And then, a couple of years later, Sergeant Dale Green was killed in the line of duty. The deaths of these two people are losses I've felt as deeply as a blood relative, maybe more so."

Andy's last career-defining moment involved another individual, a man who was my police academy classmate and coworker at the police department. In my opinion, it is a story of true selflessness, which is why I felt compelled to include it in Andy's story.

He said, "After nearly ten years as a captain in internal investigations, the Florida legislature shifted all sworn members at the Department of Environmental Protection to Fish and Wildlife. Since the bill didn't specify what would happen to our office, I was faced with either losing my law enforcement credentials, moving to the Fish and Wildlife Commission (FWC), or becoming unemployed. I had worked since I was a kid with a paperboy route. The prospect of being unemployed was foreign to me, and a major blow to my workaholic ego. The hammer fell, and I was told that only two of the four captains were going to FWC, a female and an African-American male. The Department of Environmental Protection was retaining the one with the most seniority, and I was the odd man out.

"The African-American male went to the FWC to speak with them and told them he wasn't coming. He had already retired once from law enforcement (the Tallahassee Police Department), and felt they took him only due to his race. He told them that they should have taken me, not him. This man put himself in my place, allowing me to continue my career while he faced unemployment.

"Fortunately, they found a non-sworn position for him. I'll never forget when he came into my office to tell me what he had done. He said it was the right thing to do. I had to shut my door so nobody could see the tears rolling down my face. What kind of man would sacrifice himself like that for his brother? Raiford Rollins would. There are not many men in uniform I respect more than him, and not because of this... it's just who he is." I would have to agree with Andy.

Life after Law Enforcement

After ten years with the state of Florida as a sworn officer, Andy left law enforcement for good. He was approached by a British company seeking to open business in the United States. It was a law enforcement support company using cutting-edge forensic technology to safeguard property assets and help apprehend criminals. As Andy said, "I chased the shiny object and left the State to become the company's first employee in the U.S."

Continuing to Put Away the Bad Guys

After a year with the company, that shiny object faded, and his position was eliminated. But Andy didn't just land on his feet. He said, "I stuck the landing! In what was totally a 'God-orchestrated' event, I entered my current job as the Florida Department of Children and Families (DCF) Director of the Office of Public Benefits Integrity."

While this isn't a law enforcement position, I wanted to include it in his story. Public benefits are often a hot topic of discussion, and Andy brings a different perspective to it.

These are Andy's thoughts: "I supervise more than one hundred eighty staff throughout the state of Florida dedicated to safeguarding the integrity of the public-assistance programs administered by DCF, primarily food stamps and Medicaid. I lead two bureaus, an investigative branch of non-sworn employees whose job it is to detect and prevent fraud at the front end before taxpayer money goes out the door. Our other bureau is dedicated to recovering the money for benefits lost due to waste, fraud, or abuse."

Early on, Andy told me his reason for becoming a police officer, and it was to put those who commit crimes in jail. It wasn't the often-heard response of wanting to help people, even though all cops truly want to do that. "Remember how I said I didn't become a cop to help people but to put bad guys in jail? Well, now I'm truly helping people – Florida's most vulnerable population. We protect these much-needed programs by enforcing regulations and stopping fraud.

"If we detect fraud, we refer the case to the Department of Financial Services Division of Public Assistance Fraud. They pursue criminal charges, or if possible, administrative sanctions. Due to the workload, they can only work about ten percent of what we send them. We try to pick up cases as we can and send those to administrative disqualification hearings. If the clients are found guilty, they are disqualified for periods ranging from one year to a lifetime ban. But our work isn't done; we go after the money lost.

"Getting money back is harder than it sounds. We use every tool at our disposal to get that money back, including intercepting lottery winnings and tax returns.

"Last year, our Bureau of Public Benefit Investigations conducted nearly twenty-three thousand investigations resulting in $41.5 million in cost-avoidance savings. Our Benefit Recovery Bureau processed almost twenty-nine thousand overpayment referrals and established nearly seventeen thousand claims valued at more than $43.5 million. We collected $29.4 million in taxpayer money, including $7.5 million returned to Florida. Not only did that cover the state's portion of my budget, but we actually generated revenue. Our total savings last year was $243 million, and I'm confident we've now exceeded one billion dollars in fraud deterred since I've been here, and we'll exceed $150 million recovered soon as well.

"My staff amazes me. These people do so much for the state and get paid so little. They go into the same neighborhoods I did while in uniform to interview people defrauding the program, only they don't have a uniform, a marked patrol vehicle, a gun, or a badge. They truly are the most selfless and amazing people. I am humbled and blessed to serve them. I may not understand why at times, but the Lord has put me here for a reason. I often fail, but my heart and mind are aligned. My identity is not in my work. It is by far the most stressful and difficult job I've had, but I wouldn't trade it for anything."

Hurricane Irma

When people think about natural disasters such as hurricanes, our first thoughts are of the mobilization of our first responders. When the disaster is of such magnitude, its effects are far-reaching. One such disaster was Hurricane Irma that struck Florida in 2017. It affected forty-eight of Florida's sixty-seven counties. Andy's office had to mobilize, and I felt their efforts were worth noting and commending.

This is Andy's description of their efforts. "One thing many people don't realize is the work the Department of Children and Families does when a natural disaster strikes. I've seen it from a law enforcement perspective, but nothing like when Hurricane Irma struck, impacting forty-eight counties in the state. When it did, DCF sprang into action. We mobilized our entire statewide workforce assigned to my office to man disaster benefit sites. A site would go up in an impacted county, and my staff would work the 'fraud tent.' Anyone suspected of potential fraud would be sent to us for a more in-depth interview. Since DCF had simultaneous sites going on in multiple locations across the state, we were forced to shut down our normal business operations for three months.

"Our staff would travel to a work site, arriving before six in the morning and worked until at least eight at night. This went on for forty-five days straight. These folks sacrificed time away from their families and homes to get food stamp relief to those impacted by Irma who legitimately needed it. When all was said and done, we conducted over forty-four thousand investigative interviews and stopped over $14 million in fraud. But that was just the beginning. We are still doing data analytics and identifying fraud that was issued onsite, working with our partner agencies to hold those accountable for defrauding the government and will be working to get that money back as well.

"The impact on the staff was tough to witness, and I did my best to visit every single site myself. I saw my people working outdoors in the heat and rain for fifteen hours straight. They ate food that I could barely stomach and did it without complaint. But it took a toll on all of us. I've had staff out on extended sick leave, medical leave, and lost some to early retirement. It nearly broke us, but it was the cheerful attitudes that most impressed me. I don't know how we did it, but we did it together. I genuinely love these people, and if the public knew how much they do behind the scenes... well, hopefully they do now. They're unsung heroes, all of them."

Andy asked me if I wanted to meet his employees, and I took him up on his offer. When I went to his office, he brought them all in. I was so amazed at their hard work and thanked them. They were obviously passionate about what they do.

Andy has talked about some of his favorite things about being a police officer, so I asked him what he loved most about his current position. "I have a passion for servant leadership. It's something I've been called to do my whole life and never have I been in a position to live it as I am now. I'm passionate about serving my people and about safeguarding the public-assistance programs that help our neediest population get on their feet.

"As a cop, I never lost sight that a few rotten apples didn't mean an entire community was full of criminals. A few broken windows didn't mean it's a high-crime neighborhood. It's the same way in public assistance, whether you're talking Medicaid or food stamp recipients.

"But just like in my days on the street, I'm going to be aggressive about getting those ineligible people out of the program. There is a lot more than the federal government cares to admit, but probably a lot fewer than the public suspects. I want to re-instill the public's confidence in these programs so they don't disappear. I get to do that now, whether it's helping uncover and shut down the largest food stamp trafficking fraud ring in program history or implementing new technologies to weed out identity thieves.

"I now travel the country, showing other states what we're doing. I think we're finally starting to get the federal folks to notice too. I've been to Washington D.C. to help our Secretary of the Department of Children and Families testify about our program. I've provided 'fix-it wish lists' to our federal partners. I've presented to nationwide sworn and non-sworn investigative groups on the problems, challenges, and solution efforts. Most recently, I've been able to talk to the White House about welfare reform for future farm bills.

"Maybe, just maybe, I'm having a real impact on the program. I hope and pray I'm having that kind of impact on our people."

With everyone's favorite part of their job, there is always an opposite, their least favorite, and for Andy, it was a simple response. "Politics! I never cared for office politics, internal gossip, or drama when I was in uniform, but in my current job, it's a different form of politics. I deal with internal politics and sometimes find myself at odds with the folks running the eligibility programs. Cops on the street suffer more exposure to stressful incidents. In my new role, it's prolonged exposure to political stress. I'm the 'DCF cop', and it always saddens me when someone mislabels me as such, thinking I'm 'anti-client.'

"I'm not. I'm 'anti-fraudster.' There's a difference, and some have trouble seeing it. I feel that way most often when dealing with the federal government. Fraud should never be just the cost of doing business, ever. I know we'll never stop it all, but we can't afford to put politics and political correctness above our mission to help those in need and run this taxpayer-funded program the right way."

Andy also finds the time to volunteer for his church when he's not at work. "I've been on our Board of Deacons for seven years now, and I help with a bi-monthly food pantry that our church members fund. It's an opportunity for me to counsel and pray with the poor and vulnerable members of our community and to help them find ways to better their circumstances. I've also been to the Amazon rainforest with A Doctor's Heart to help build a children's church in a river community."

He's also found an enjoyable hobby. "I enjoy a good craft beer, especially if it's one I've made. I have a few close friends who I brew with and have had a blast doing it. Maybe it's the Irish in me. But there's nothing better than serving your beer to someone else and seeing them enjoy it too!

"I've brewed for fundraisers such as Pints for Paws, raising money for animal shelters. A good friend and I have won the best beer 'People's Choice' award, and one of our local breweries serves one of my recipes."

Andy also has a passion for his Florida State University Seminoles and works as a photographer's assistant on the field for football games. He describes that experience simply: "It's so much fun!"

I asked Andy if he had any thoughts he'd like to pass on. "Cops are people, full of flaws like the rest of us. But they all possess two important traits: an uncanny bravery to run toward trouble and a willingness to serve and protect others to their own detriment. We need the public's support, to be held accountable for the tasks assigned to us, to be given the tools to do the job, and most importantly, we need their prayers.

A Shadow Box of Badges

"I still have my law enforcement credentials with the Leon County Sheriff's Office, but I don't practice it. My career spanned nearly two decades, and I'm now left with a shadow box of badges I've worn and scars that are mostly healed.

"To my fellow law enforcement officers with whom I have served, I thank you. Thank you for the friendships, the brotherhood, for protecting my life more times than I can count, and most importantly, for the laughs. And know this, my friends, there is life beyond the badge!"

Most importantly, Andy said, "Without a doubt, I couldn't tell my story without including the most important parts of me, my smart and beautiful wife Tricia, our son Ryan, and my God.

"Our son Ryan is an amazing young man who is smart, good-looking, kind, and passionate. He's a straight-A student, a talented musician, and aspires to be a surgeon. He graduated high school this year; I'm so proud of him and can't wait to see the man he grows into as he begins his college experience and his journey toward his chosen career."

Andy, thank you for your heartfelt thoughts and for your service. I have no doubt that you are making a difference.

Special Agent Alan Lopez

**Tallahassee Police Department: Seven Years
United States Drug Enforcement Administration: Twenty-One Years
Retired: Twenty-Eight Years of Service**

I met Alan early in his career when he was hired at the Tallahassee Police Department. He was one of our agency's first Hispanic officers. Like many, Alan's initial career plans did not involve becoming a police officer, and eventually he left local law enforcement to make a career at a federal agency. Many people forget about our federal officers when talking about law enforcement. While they may not face the everyday calls for service, they deal with different dangers, and many have lost their lives in the line of duty. I wanted to bring attention to our federal officers and honor their service. Having Alan agree to let me share his story is also an honor.

Alan graduated from Florida State University in 1985, with his bachelor of science degree in criminology. He entered law school in 1986. He said, "Law school convinced me that a law degree wasn't going to satisfy my career goals or my thirst for adventure. I realized what interested me in the criminal justice system was to be actively involved in fighting crime and not an attorney behind a desk, dealing with issues in court after the events had transpired."

A Lengthy Process

In late 1987 and early 1988, Alan applied for jobs with federal law enforcement agencies, and he received some employment offers. He explained, "The application process consisted of passing a written exam, in-depth interviews with a panel of the organization's senior managers, a physical fitness test that measured your aptitude for strength and endurance, a medical exam, a drug test, a polygraph, and passing a thorough background investigation in order to obtain a top-secret clearance. The background investigation alone averaged twelve to eighteen months to complete, making the entire hiring process quite lengthy.

"One federal recruiter, a former police officer, recommended that in the meantime, I try to work for a municipal police department to gain experience at the local level. One of my college professors spoke highly of the Tallahassee Police Department (TPD), its professional accreditation credentials, and that TPD required a college degree for employment. He agreed with the recruiter's recommendation and advised me to apply."

Alan was hired by the Tallahassee Police Department and began the police academy in 1988. Upon graduation, he was assigned to a field training squad. He said, "My initial plan was to hire on for two years at the most before moving onto a federal agency. However, I enjoyed local policing and the agency so much that when a federal agency I had applied to called to finalize the job offer two years later, I declined to accept.

"One of the contingencies for most federal agencies when hiring is signing and accepting a mobility agreement stipulating that once hired, you'll be reassigned to a location that meets the agency's needs. It could be anywhere in the United States. The thought of leaving my friends, coworkers, and the Tallahassee community and possibly being assigned to offices in Detroit or New York City was not very enticing."

He spent the next six and a half years working the road as a patrol officer, three and a half years as a field training officer.

About two years into his career, Alan had a discussion with his shift lieutenant. It started out as a counseling session about a call for service he had responded to, but that conversation revisited the possibility of working at the federal level.

Things Not to Do While on Light Duty

He explained, "Approximately two years into my career at TPD, I was called into the Watch Commander's Office where I was 'counseled' by my shift lieutenant for responding to a domestic violence call while on light duty. I had been working the nightshift in the duty office after fracturing my ankle. That evening, I was given permission to leave the front desk and get a bite to eat. While returning from the restaurant, an emergency call came through from dispatch about an armed domestic violence case in progress. No other units were available, so I and my dining buddy (another TPD officer) responded to the call.

"There were two suspects in the residence, and we were the first unit to arrive. I was in plain clothes with a cast on my right foot to just below the knee. We entered the apartment and detained the two suspects. Before we could turn the incident over to the patrol unit and return to the station, my shift lieutenant arrived at the scene. She was not happy. She directed me back to the station where she enlightened me on city liability issues dealing with light-duty officers responding to high-risk calls.

"Luckily, the lieutenant was always firm but also fair and approachable. She also used the time to inquire of my career goals. I told her about the federal positions I had been offered and declined and that my current goal was to remain at TPD in Tallahassee. She provided me with career-advancement advice to include furthering my education and law enforcement career. The lieutenant encouraged me to not shut out the possibility of employment with a federal agency. As someone who was fluent in Spanish, a federal job could provide an opportunity to work in many countries throughout the world. That conversation stayed imprinted in the back of my mind. Five years later, that conversation provided me with validation/encouragement to leave local law enforcement and venture into the federal level."

Alan mentioned another situation that reiterated his desire to achieve more out of his career. "I was involved in the pursuit of a stolen vehicle, running with my lights and sirens. We were headed north past the city limits on US Highway 27. A K9 unit was my back up, the traffic was light, and the weather conditions were clear. As we were passing Lake Jackson, I thought to myself, *There's no reason for the sergeant or the watch commander to cancel this pursuit.* I was certain the suspect would not get away, and we were going to make the arrest.

"As we passed Capital Circle, two Leon County Sheriff's Deputies joined the pursuit. Shortly thereafter, the watch commander relayed through dispatch that we were to terminate the pursuit, citing it was outside the city limits and outside our jurisdiction. Needless to say, we were not too happy. The suspect was arrested, but TPD was not involved. It brought home the fact that local law enforcement has limited jurisdictional authority. For me, that sucked and made me realize that I (still) wanted more out of my career."

During this time, Alan tried out for a position on the department's Hostage Negotiation Team and was chosen. It wasn't an easy process. "The tryouts were intense. It began with an oral interview. Next were the physical fitness and tactical tryouts. There were many candidates who applied. I was proud to be one of the chosen.

"The camaraderie and lifelong friendships that developed with the team members were life-changing. The training received as a member of the TAC (SWAT) Team was phenomenal. We trained to handle all types of high-stress/critical situations from domestic violence to terrorist activities. One particular requirement that became a staple for all negotiators was provided by Florida State University and the regional Crisis Helpline. This training altered the way I identified and interacted with individuals who were under extreme stress and/or mentally ill.

Trained to Listen

"The training focused on becoming an active listener. It taught me how to truly listen to what the person was saying, to identify the crippling stress they felt and attempt to help that person. To say this type of training was not natural for me is an understatement. Prior to this training, my natural response was to identify the problem and handle it swiftly by placing the person under arrest or by Baker Acting them. (Law enforcement is allowed to commit an individual to a mental-health facility under the Florida Mental Health Act of 1971 and is commonly known as the Baker Act.)

"The training taught me to listen in a way I never understood before. I've always heard what a person was saying but didn't listen to the meaning behind the words. The training was intense; in all it totaled several hundred hours, including time counseling on a crisis hot line. As a police officer, you're trained to read body language, to see someone's facial and eye expressions. Over the phone, all you have to interpret is a voice, inflection, and the spoken words."

Alan and I shared one assignment that lasted three weeks. We responded to Miami, Florida, in 1992, two days after Hurricane Andrew devastated South Florida. In Alan's words, "We deployed to South Florida to assist with recovery. I got to witness firsthand the devastation Mother Nature unleashed on those residents. It created shock throughout the entire community, including to the first responders who were personally affected by the disaster. That experience never leaves you.

During my time with the Drug Enforcement Administration (DEA), I never deployed to a natural disaster, but other agents did. After Hurricane Katrina, many special agents and fingerprint specialists assisted local agencies to restore order, some normalcy, and help identify the deceased.

Foreign Affairs

"However, I responded to other parts of the world where disasters were manmade. Entering a village where narcoterrorists had recently killed all members of the local law enforcement agency, then ransacked the homes of the villagers, was excruciating. When you speak to the widows and surviving coworkers, it tears you up inside. You want to help and protect these people, but you know when you leave, they're back at the mercy of these thugs.

"The local and federal governments are usually too weak or inept to protect these people. At least in the snapshot of the time, we were there, and they felt some comfort of protection. Those situations would bring me back to the time in South Florida when the community was devastated, but the full force of the local and federal government was there to help. The services provided might sometimes be slow to arrive, but they would arrive. That's what makes this country so wonderful and why so many people throughout the world dream of coming here. If anyone doubts how great we have it here, try living and relying on the services in other countries. We are truly blessed to live in the United States."

Career progression at TPD landed Alan into the Criminal Investigation Division and assigned to the joint Auto Theft Task Force. This task force combined personnel with our sister agency, the Leon County Sheriff's Office.

These were Alan's thoughts: "Not that I felt unfulfilled at TPD; it was that I wanted more out of my law enforcement career. I wanted to experience being stationed in other parts of the country and perhaps other parts of the world. I wanted to see how it's done elsewhere with more resources, training, and funding. I just wanted to experience more.

The DEA

"When researching federal agencies, I zeroed in on the Drug Enforcement Administration (DEA) for its mission to target drug traffickers and their assets. There are DEA offices throughout the United States and the world. The DEA was a great organization for me. It's the world's leading drug enforcement agency that deals with the most corrupt and evil substances decaying society. The DEA has over five thousand special agents whose goal is to dismantle the most notorious high-level drug trafficking and terrorist organizations threatening the United States."

He continued, "Being born and raised in Miami, Florida, I saw firsthand how the wonderful town I grew up in became a violent, drug-infested city almost overnight. The number of shootings, homicides, robberies, and burglaries skyrocketed, all because of illegal drugs.

"Domestically, DEA offices identify and gather evidence on as many members of drug trafficking organizations as possible in their geographic areas of responsibilities. The investigations continue in order to tie those organizations to their foreign source of supply. The DEA foreign offices target narcotraffickers throughout the world, the ones who control the cartels and major criminal terrorist organizations. Most, if not all, terrorist organizations fund their operations with drug proceeds.

"Between domestic and foreign investigations, DEA is able to apply and obtain extradition orders for the most powerful drug traffickers in the world. These individuals have so much money and influence in their countries that they are almost fearless in the consequences of their trade. Their only fear is an extradition order to the U.S."

In 1996, Alan was hired by the Drug Enforcement Administration as a special agent and left the Tallahassee Police Department. The hiring process is thorough and in-depth. "In my case, it took more than a year to complete. Any employment offer was contingent on passing every step of the hiring process."

Alan said that training with DEA is an ongoing process. "It starts at the DEA Academy in Quantico, Virginia, where it's eighteen weeks long. You're trained in various aspects of federal law enforcement to include firearms, tactical skills, financial investigations, Title 21 laws, undercover operations, communication intercepts, ethics, leadership, and field procedures and techniques.

"Depending on where you're deployed or stationed, that could require additional training. During my twenty-one-plus years with the DEA, I was stationed in North Florida, Central California, South America, Alaska, the DEA Academy, Southwest Asia, and Alabama. Being stationed in South America required special training on how to conduct operations in the jungles of the Amazon. Stationed in Southwest Asia required specialized desert training, survival training, and advanced first-aid and trauma training.

"Domestically, in the Central Valley in California, specialized training in clandestine laboratory operations was required due to all the super Mexican labs that included meth and pseudoephedrine reduction labs in the region. Cold weather operational training was necessary for Alaska.

"Training continues throughout your career as traffickers change their methods, thus the DEA trains to detect and combat those changes. For example, at the beginning of my time with the DEA, traffickers used pagers and pay phones to communicate. Now, it's cell phones, satellite phones, GPS, and computers just like the rest of the world."

I asked Alan about work schedules and conditions for DEA agents, and he told me, "As an agent, you're expected to work as long as it's needed. Most good agents I encountered throughout my career worked long hours through significant family events and holidays. There were cases that required extended stationary surveillance that evolved into mobile surveillance, which required travel to an adjoining city and then evolved into air travel to another state.

The Life of a DEA Agent

"On one such case, it was six days with little sleep before I was able to return home for a day. The next day, I returned to work to continue on the case. This is the prelude to the life of an agent, to expect the unexpected, adapt, and OVERCOME.

"My partner and his wife were expecting their first born: twins. They were not due for at least a month. The case required us to travel out of state to interview a source of information. The trip was expected to last just a couple of days; however, after the initial interview, there was more to follow up on, and we had to extend the trip.

"The night before our return, my partner's wife was experiencing discomfort, nothing to worry about, as we were traveling back the following day. In typical agent fashion, we were running late to make our departure because of last-minute calls and meeting with local agents. We barely arrived in time to board the flights (pre-9/11 and TSA). We had no cell phones, just pagers, so we couldn't call the office or home for any updates. Immediately upon arrival, a customs agent traveling with us received an urgent call for my partner to call the office ASAP.

"When he did, he was instructed to head to the hospital because his wife was in labor. I had driven to the airport, and my vehicle was in the parking lot. We ran to the car and discovered that the left rear tire was almost flat. Luckily, it had enough air in it to go a short distance We decided to take a chance and drove to the gas station across the street from the airport.

"Over the customs agent's cell phone, we were told not to worry and that another agent was with her in the delivery room. The distance from the airport to the hospital was approximately eight miles. Not wanting my partner to miss out on the birth of his children, I drove as if I was responding to a robbery in progress.

"The government vehicle had a siren, but the emergency lights weren't functioning. I drove in excess of the speed limit, with only the siren on. When we were about halfway there, we noticed a fire truck running with lights and siren in the left lane; however, it was driving too slowly for our needs, so I passed it on the right. When we arrived at the hospital, I dropped my partner off at the front entrance and parked my government vehicle in the first available spot, which was far from the entrance.

Stopped by the Cops

"When I exited the vehicle, I was immediately surrounded by numerous police cruisers from the local department. They didn't draw their weapons but forcefully requested that I raise my hands and inquired why I was driving so aggressively through their city and why I passed the fire truck.

"After identifying myself as a DEA Special Agent and providing a thorough explanation of the situation, the sergeant at the scene gave me a royal tongue-lashing on the proper procedures for emergency driving in their city, went on to cite all the traffic codes I violated, and how they could haul me in to see a judge. I told them I understood, and he had every right to do so, but if my partner arrived in time to see the birth of his kids, it would be worth it.

"The sergeant was extremely professional and let me off with a warning. He then added humorously, "I would have done the same thing and passed those hose draggers to get to the hospital." Fortunately for all, my partner was able to be with his wife and witness the birth of his son and daughter, and I didn't go to jail. It was one of the shining moments of my career.

"To add more stress to this already stressful job, shortly after my partner's wife gave birth to their twins, we were back on another case involving a wire intercept assist in identifying drug load deliveries. My partner and I worked sixty-three days, averaging twelve- to sixteen-hour work days with only one day off. My partner was running the wire-room, and I was running surveillance. All the brownie points I had earned for getting my partner to the delivery room on time were now null and void."

The Politics of the Job

I asked Alan to tell me what, for him, was the most difficult part of his job. He said, "Politics! The politics among offices, departments, agencies, governments, and countries is what makes the job the most difficult. As a local law enforcement officer, I saw the difference between the police department and the sheriff's department. When I started in the Criminal Investigation Division, we were exposed to a federal agency's way of dealing with cases solved by locals. They would call a press conference and then take credit for how the case was solved without ever mentioning or crediting the hard work done by the local law enforcement agency.

"Politics in international cases were even more complex. When we, as investigators, prove that a suspect is a drug trafficker, member or leader of a terrorist group, murderer, rapist, money launderer, and/or a kidnapper, a host country might classify these individuals as outstanding members of society.

"In some countries, groups and members of these narcoterrorist organizations are given amnesty for all their crimes. They're allowed to return to society if they promise to behave. All is forgiven; all the murdered officers, soldiers, widows, victims, and orphans remain dead or victimized, and the bad guys get a pass, all because some politicians decide it's best.

"At times, decisions are handed down by division heads to the agents, telling them that the targets of the agent's investigations would not be extradited from their country even if the United States issued an extradition order. This makes my blood boil. On a case you've invested an enormous amount of time in, including nights and holidays, as well as having been exposed to danger, and now for some politician or non-law enforcement agency to close down the case, was extremely difficult to accept. You remember all the victims and their families, and realize that for them, justice will never be served. Many times, we would vent to each other that dealing with criminals was the easiest part of our job."

There are always positives to a career in law enforcement, so I asked Alan what was the most rewarding part of his job. He responded, "I had a wonderful career with DEA. I was able to accomplish more in law enforcement than I ever dreamed of. I had cases that took me to so many places throughout the world. I conducted enforcement operations in just about every venue imaginable: jungle operations in the Amazon of South America, marijuana eradication in the Sierra Mountains, clandestine lab seizures in Alaska, surveillance operations in war-torn regions of Southwest Asia, and undercover assignments in numerous capacities.

"I was extremely fortunate to work with some of the most elite international organizations as well as some of the United States' best: Delta, SEAL, Special Forces Teams, Coast Guard, and Air Force.

"Looking back, one of my biggest career accomplishments was being the case agent in the indictment of a narcoterrorist organization shortly after 9/11. As a matter of fact, my partner was scheduled to brief the DEA Administrator at headquarters about our case when he observed the plane crash into the Pentagon building on 9/11.

Developing irrefutable evidence through hundreds of hours of travel and countless interviews and interrogations, resulting in indictments and arrests of members of a narcoterrorist organization, became a shining moment in my career. Investigating a terrorist organization, which assailed itself as a riotous, left-wing, political organization attempting to become the government of a country, and then exposing this group as just a bunch of greedy, murderous drug-trafficking thugs was extremely satisfying."

Killed in the Line of Duty

I also asked if Alan could provide me with what he felt was his career-defining moment. He shared this: "During the first week of the police academy, I met a TPD officer with a large smile and a wonderful laugh. I spoke to him for fewer than ten minutes. He was gracious, funny, and helpful. He offered me a few pointers to get through the academy and told me to call him if I needed anything. He also had a Spanish last name.

"Within a week, that officer was gunned down by prison escapees from another state. His death affected me more than I could comprehend at the time. Someone whom I had just met, in the same profession I was pursuing, was killed on a call for service. That was unimaginable and tragic.

"Dealing with the death of a fellow law enforcement officer I've worked with, regardless of the uniform they wore or the country they worked for, has always been the most difficult. Years later, I remembered the last conversations I had with them. Had I known it would be the last, I would have added to that conversation just how much their friendship meant. It's never gotten easier, and to this day I've never gotten over such loss. I've somewhat learned to deal with it and go on by honoring their memory and attempting to complete what they were denied finishing."

As with most in law enforcement, the importance of family and the sacrifices they make are undeniable. These are Alan's thoughts: "Family has always been a very important factor in my life. The support they have provided is immeasurable. I know I would not have been able to accomplish as much as I did without knowing they were supportive of me.

Family Life with the DEA

"One of the first personally important tasks I undertook upon joining the DEA was completing a will and increasing my life insurance policy in case something unfortunate happened. It gave me great peace of mind to know my family would be taken care of financially. Every time I took a hazardous assignment, I increased the value of the payout. If my wife knew how much the payout was on my last overseas tour, she might have considered contracting someone to wipe me out.

"Being away from home was always difficult. I dealt with the separation by reminding myself that I was doing something for the greater good. I always believed that our mission was righteous and important to the country. However, it was extremely difficult for those left behind. I can only imagine how they felt, not knowing where I was at times and not being able to see me come home at the end of the day. It was a sacrifice not being involved in their lives.

"When deployed overseas, you are at the mercy of third-world technology to communicate with loved ones back home. Sometimes it works, but most times it doesn't. When I was able to get a call through to home, I could tell when something in my general area had made the news because the tone in my wife's voice was pure relief.

"During my first overseas deployment to South America, my mother would listen to every available Spanish news station to see if there were any incidents in the area where I was stationed. If the country was mentioned, she would call my sister, worried for my safety or concerned that something had happened. My sister or brother-in-law would call my wife, who would then contact me and tell me to call my mother as soon as possible to reassure her everything was fine. My parents were never told the location of my last overseas assignment. I guess (or more accurately, I've been told) the stress put on my family was much different from the stresses I experienced while doing what I enjoyed."

Lastly, I asked Alan if he had any thoughts that he'd like to share with folks outside the law enforcement life. He said, "Being a DEA agent or a police officer is not just a job. It is our life and our families' lives. It can be personally restrictive. We must be guarded and careful of who we allow into our lives. We can't, nor would we, associate with known felons. We also can't socialize with casual or illicit drug users or socialize with non-vetted foreign nationals who could jeopardize our security clearance. Same goes with associating with doctors or pharmaceutical officials who are under investigation.

"It was a satisfying career, lots of highs and some lows but very fulfilling. It demanded great sacrifices personally and from my family. I spent great lengths of time being separated from them. In the beginning of my DEA career, technology wasn't what it is today with cell phone service and things such as Face Time or Skype, so contact with them was often minimal. Later in my career, as technology grew, the ability to communicate with them more frequently helped tremendously."

Alan, thank you for your service to your community and to your country.

Lieutenant Lee Majors

Aviation Section Commander
Leon County Sheriff's Office
Active Duty: Eighteen Years of Service

I knew of Lee several years before I actually met him. I was working at the Tallahassee Police Department (TPD), and Lee was with our sister agency, the Leon County Sheriff's Office (LCSO), as a member of its Aviation Section. Oftentimes they would assist TPD, and he was our voice and eyes in the sky. Just prior to my retirement in 2006, I became friends with his wife Angel and finally met Lee.

When thinking of whom I wanted in this book, Lee quickly came to mind. His path to a career in law enforcement is different from most. As I've learned, being a member of an aviation unit requires an abundance of training and skill. Both are things I thought people should know.

I asked Lee why he chose a law enforcement career, and he told me this: "I can't say that I necessarily chose to be in law enforcement. I can't say I'd dreamed of being a police officer since I was a kid like so many others. Law enforcement, and aviation in particular, turned out to be where I could use my unique experience, abilities, and training to be a part of the solution to problems in our community instead of being part of the problem. Solving problems, logistics planning, completing complex technical tasks, flying, and forward thinking to stay one step ahead are all things I enjoy and are part of my everyday job."

In 1985, Lee joined the Leon County Sheriff's Office CB Posse. This was a volunteer group that helped monitor CB Channel Nine for emergency traffic and assisted the agency in an unarmed, uniformed capacity with special events. It is now called the Auxiliary Posse and no longer deals with CB radios. He also volunteered with another organization, and between the two, allowed Lee to "tie together my technical abilities with my desire to serve."

Aviation Unit

In 1989, Lee obtained his auxiliary officer credentials and was introduced to the captain supervising the Aviation Unit. He began volunteering time with it and began doing nonpilot flight officer duties. While volunteering with the unit, he earned his private airplane rating on his own.

Lee then approached the captain with a proposal for LCSO to provide training for his commercial helicopter transition. He said, "I thought I could then fill vacant shifts and take care of weekend community displays, special details, and other functions providing the full-time members some staffing relief." The sheriff approved the idea and paid for some of his helicopter training, but not all of it. His other training and licensing came at his own expense. Lee had spent a total of fifteen years as an unpaid auxiliary officer.

In January of 2000, Lee started with the Aviation Unit full-time. He owned his own business as well and had decided that "the stress of owning my own business had become too much, and it was time to do something else." At that same time, the captain of the Unit decided to retire, which created an opening.

Lee expressed an interest in becoming a full-time member of this elite unit. With the help of the captain and the approval of the sheriff, he was hired into the Aviation Unit. In 2001, he graduated from the police academy with his full law enforcement credentials.

A Helicopter Pilot in Law Enforcement

I asked Lee to explain the process to becoming a helicopter pilot and how it relates to a law enforcement Aviation Unit. It's rather lengthy, but I felt it important to include. He explained, "There are generally two ways to receive flight training—military and private. Military, of course, affords you some of the best flight training in the world, but the commitment and lifestyle are not for everyone.

"Civilian training can generally be conducted at your own pace but is fairly expensive. Aviation-specific degrees can be obtained at several colleges. To be employable in private or government aviation, a minimum of a commercial license and an instrument pilot certificate is usually required.

"Starting from scratch, you would receive your private pilot's certificate. FAA requirements include forty hours of flight time. You would be an exceptional student to be ready in forty-eight hours for a check ride or flying with an instructor as a kind of in-flight test; fifty to sixty hours would probably be closer to the norm. There are no specific requirements for the amount of ground instruction with an instructor, but I would estimate forty to fifty hours.

"In addition to this, you'll spend many, many more hours than that studying on your own. You then have to pass a written exam, an oral exam, and a flight test to receive your first certificate. With your new private pilot certificate, you can legally fly for pleasure but not for hire.

"Generally, you would then start working on your instrument rating. This prepares you to fly without visual reference to the ground. Think inside clouds or minimal weather conditions. Flight instruction, ground instruction, self-study, written exam, oral exam, and a flight test again. But you still can't fly for hire, so you start working on your commercial certificate.

"Commercial training prepares you to operate within much tighter tolerances with a higher level of understanding since you'll be responsible for passengers. Again, there is flight and ground training, self-study, written and oral exams, and a flight test. So now with your new commercial certificate, you are employable.

"But wait; you may only have a couple hundred hours of flight time, far less than the fifteen hundred to two thousand hours many potential employers require. Many people build their flight time doing flight instruction. The flight training industry is one of the few places where your first job can be as an instructor.

"So now you need an instructor's certificate and probably an instrument instructor's certificate. Of course, more flight and ground instruction, self-study, written and oral exams, and flight tests.

"At this point, you may have invested several years, and easily the cost of a fine college education, to get your first job as a flight instructor, which allows you to build enough flight time to move onto a more lucrative job. There are exceptions to this. In the law enforcement segment of the market, depending on the size of the agency, candidates may be identified within the agency and receive their flight training in-house. In fact, it's common.

"Having worked with civilian pilots hired into law enforcement and law enforcement officers who were trained to be pilots, I prefer the latter. Not every police officer is an appropriate candidate to be a pilot; in fact, very few are, but having a police mindset makes one better at what we do.

"At our agency, we have trained pilots from within and hired very accomplished law enforcement pilots from outside our agency, depending on the need at the time. Positions in any aviation unit are few compared to the rest of the agency and don't open very often. Competition can be fierce. Having the right attitude and mindset can often be more valuable than a pocket full of licenses.

"This doesn't take into account the fact that, with few exceptions, you'll be required to hold law enforcement certification as well. With LCSO, some of our pilots also hold aerial applicator certificates as we do aerial mosquito control for the county."

Aviation Certifications and Licenses

I asked Lee what other aircraft he's licensed to fly besides helicopters. He said "I hold an Airline Transport Pilot certificate, which is the highest level of pilot certification obtainable. I have privileges in helicopters, single-engine land and sea airplanes, multi-engine airplanes, and unmanned aerial systems (drones). I also hold flight instructor's certificates in helicopters and single-engine airplanes as well as instrument instructor privileges in helicopters and airplanes."

While law enforcement officers often have required yearly training and updates, Lee and the other pilots in his unit also have other flight mandates to keep their licenses current. They're required to do both.

He explained what's required. "Pilot's certificates don't expire. The only training required to exercise the privileges are that you complete a flight review with an instructor every two years. To fly commercially, however, you have to renew your second-class FAA medical certificate every year.

"As you age, this of course becomes more troublesome. The exam itself, conducted by an FAA-designated physician, isn't particularly difficult. The problem is that any time you go to your family doctor for anything, you run the risk of a diagnosis that would be career-ending or at least ground you until further testing and documentation can be reviewed. This often takes months or years, depending on the condition. Many medications prescribed for common conditions are not allowed by the FAA. Physical and mental fitness are a must for an extended career in aviation.

"Most law enforcement aviation units do a lot of in-house training. At LCSO, we practice emergency flight procedures every three months, airborne use of force every six months, and night-vision flight procedures every two months. We train for care track (radio tracking of dementia patients) at least once a year, and conduct instrument flight procedures routinely, just to name a few types of trainings and practices we must undergo. Flight instructors have requirements for training and recertification every two years, and those who hold aerial applicators' licenses (mosquito control) have continuing education requirements to exercise those privileges.

"Those things are unit-specific, and then add on all the standard law enforcement recurrent annual training/retraining. Routine training has a prominent place in any well-established law enforcement aviation unit."

Action from the Sky

Most people see aviation units in the media, mostly when they assist with high-speed vehicle pursuits, disaster rescues, or with searches of wanted violent felons. They do so much more, so I asked Lee to give a detailed explanation of what a law enforcement pilot and aviation unit do.

He said, "The duties of a law enforcement pilot vary widely depending on what the focus of your agency is. To oversimplify it, we use our unique elevated position to observe and report what we see.

"A highway patrol pilot may spend most of his time monitoring traffic and doing speed measurement. A pilot with a wildlife conservation agency may spend a lot of time searching for game poachers, wildlife violations both over land and water, or searching for overdue boaters or hunters.

"In an agency like LCSO, the missions vary widely, but our primary focus is supporting deputies or police officers on the ground in the execution of their duties. It could be looking for unusual activity in a high-crime area or the pursuit of fleeing suspects on foot or in a car, searching for lost or missing people, boats, or airplanes, flying cover for dignitary movement, inserting SWAT assets, storm damage assessment, or crime scene photography, as well as other tasks.

"Often when an arrest warrant is being served on a violent suspect, we have to provide not only information on the location before the arrest team arrives, but we also have to be prepared to track anyone who might attempt to flee. Additionally, we do power line patrol and mosquito control.

"The aircraft we fly today are equipped with an extensive suite of electronic sensors and equipment to help us do our job. Thermal imagers and night vision, or light amplification devices, allow us to see in the dark. Powerful cameras and gyro-stabilized binoculars allow us to see from a distance. However, none of the information we gather is much good if we can't talk to deputies or officers on the ground, so an extensive suite of powerful radios and communication gear has become standard equipment on most law enforcement aircraft.

"The job has become very technical, with advancements in the equipment we carry onboard. Because of our unique ability to see the bigger picture of a complex situation or being able to provide information while not being in the heat of battle on the ground, we often take over the role of command and control of a situation.

"It's not uncommon for the air crew to use all their equipment to position multiple officers and deputies on the ground during a search or pursuit. At the same time, we coordinate with several other agencies by radio in an attempt to stay several steps ahead of a suspect. And just as fast-paced and unpredictable as the duties of a road deputy are, our workload, stress, and danger can change drastically in an instant."

The Leon County Sheriff's Office currently has seven hundred nineteen employees. Five hundred thirteen are sworn deputies, two hundred twenty-eight are corrections officers, and two hundred ten are civilians. The Aviation Unit is staffed with seven people: six are pilots/tactical flight officers and one is its full-time mechanic. These seven positions have very specific responsibilities.

The Flight Crew

Lee said, "Generally, the flight crew consists of two people: the pilot and the tactical flight officer or TFO. The pilot's job is to fly the aircraft where the TFO needs it to be to do their job. That includes communicating with air traffic control and other aircraft, dealing with weather and air traffic, and being ready for any emergency at all times.

"The TFO has the hard job, managing all of the onboard technology, such as cameras, thermal imager or FLIR (Forward Looking InfraRed), search light, mission management computer, and multiple radios. It's normal for us to monitor seven radios simultaneously. The TFO is the one who does most of the work managing a scene or incident, placing perimeter units, and tracking suspects or vehicles. In our unit, everyone is cross-trained to do both jobs so the coordination between the two positions and between the aircraft and ground units is very dynamic.

"Perhaps, though, one of the most overlooked and most critical positions is our mechanic. Without an airworthy aircraft, nobody else can do their job. Most people don't understand that the job of the mechanic isn't just changing oil and turning wrenches. A large part of their job is also managing the timing of extensive and complex maintenance items so aircraft are always available."

Natural Disaster Rescues

Living in Florida, natural disasters such as hurricanes are a yearly threat. First responders do so much more during such disasters, and most often must leave their families and homes to ride out the storms. They can't evacuate; they have a variety of critical jobs to help their communities recover. As you've read, aviation units are some of the most highly trained and skilled units in any law enforcement agency. While rescues are the most visible tasks performed, there is so much more.

Lee explained what his unit does during hurricanes. "Because of our unique ability to provide rapid, wide-area damage assessment and rescue, aviation assets are usually some of the first responders deployed to natural disasters. During one of our last hurricanes, the eye of the storm passed over us and caused large-scale power outages in the city. Many of these were trees on power distribution lines between generating stations and substations that stretch across three counties.

"There were fifteen circuits offline, and by regulation, every foot of each line has to be visually inspected before it can be put back online. The request for air support came near five a.m. At eight a.m., the wind had calmed down enough to safely take off. We inspected all the lines and reported our findings within a few hours. This would have taken multiple teams all day by truck.

"We've all seen television news reports of helicopters rescuing people after Hurricane Katrina and other similar events. What most people don't see is that after one of these events, the initial response is just the beginning of our work. Roadways that have to be cleared need to be identified so that emergency vehicles can pass, patrolling areas that may be without power where residents have evacuated and looking for looters are routine. Doing damage assessment and reporting is critical as FEMA and other agencies begin ramping up their response.

"If a hurricane is threatening a near landfall, we may evacuate our aircraft out of harm's way and return as soon as the worst of the weather has passed. While most people prepare a day or two before a hurricane threatens, my preparations begin a week prior to the expected impact. It also means I may not be with my family if they have to evacuate or ride out a storm at home. In general, when a storm is approaching, I pack to be away from home for days as we could be deployed to other areas where our services are needed."

Sacrifices Made

Lee's mention of the potential for being away from family and home for days is true for many first responders in disaster situations. They also have the daily aspect of shift work, which often means rotating between daytime hours, afternoon hours, midnight hours, weekends, and holidays.

Lee explained what his work life is like for himself and the other members of the Aviation Unit. "My agency is a medium-sized agency, and we often have to do more with fewer people.

That's usually the way it is with most specialty teams in the agency such as SWAT, Hostage Negotiations, and our dive team, to name a few.

"You have to be flexible with your schedule. I work daytime hours four days a week and a night shift one day and usually one or two Saturdays each month. All members of the Aviation Unit have to bounce back and forth between day and night shift. Because of our involvement in so many different things, our schedule is subject to change on a moment's notice.

"Working longer than expected on an operation often means having to make arrangements at the last minute. My wife works full-time, so sometimes we would have to find someone to pick up the kids. I've missed events or often showed up late.

"Since we don't have enough personnel for a twenty-four-hour operation, everyone is expected to be on call. This is one of the difficult parts of the job. Being awakened from a sound sleep, driving with lights and siren across the county, and then taking off into the pitch-black night to go to the next county to search for a fleeing felon in the span of forty minutes is like going from zero to one hundred in seconds. If you're someone who needs to plan your calendar in advance and can't tolerate when it's disrupted, this job isn't for you.

"Because of the strain I know this puts on family life, as a supervisor I encourage my employees to take their personal leave time and get away. When they're off, I do everything I can to not have to call them. We make every effort to accommodate team members' personal needs as much as possible. Should anyone have a family emergency, by all means it comes first."

Those thoughts tie into what Lee considers to be the toughest part of his job. While the priority is the job they have to do, he tries to ensure that his employees are happy and motivated. He said, "As a supervisor, the hardest part for me is dealing with the different personalities within my team.

Everyone on my team is strong, Type-A people by design. They must be self-motivated, confident, and able to take charge without hesitation.

"However, their different personalities don't always agree, and I'm the one they look to for decisions and guidance. In many cases, a healthy discussion will resolve a conflict. Our job is difficult and stressful enough without conflict, and I try to resolve things quickly. In some cases, nothing needs to be done, and the team member feels better after having told me of the situation or asking for direction. Decisions made department-wide or within the unit don't always please everyone. The thing that keeps me up at night is when I know someone is unhappy at work."

For Lee, the most rewarding part of his job is very simple: "Using my unique talents and abilities to be part of the solution in our community, not being part of the problem. Finding a lost child or a dementia patient and bringing them home, finding the suspect who has eluded other officers and bringing them to justice, and making sure the suspect fleeing justice doesn't get away without having to answer for their actions. These things are part of why I love my job."

Family First...Always

I ask everyone in my books to tell me what they feel is their career-defining moment, and everyone has at least one. Lee's is a bit different and really isn't job-related. This is how he described it: "We all have experiences that most will never be exposed to in their jobs. Many of these would certainly be life-changing moments to most people, but they become part of the job to us. What I think has defined my leadership philosophy as much as anything else had nothing to do with the job.

"In early 2014, I was attempting to position myself for promotion to sergeant in the Aviation Section. I was unhappy with the way the unit was going. I felt I had to be a part of the solution if I was going to stay with it and be happy. Unfortunately, during this time, my wife Angel became seriously ill. After many visits to specialists and numerous hospital stays, she was sent by ambulance to the Mayo Clinic in Jacksonville, Florida.

"I filled out my required Family Medical Leave Act paperwork and left town to be with her. While it wasn't something I dwelled on, I had to wonder if my absence of unknown duration would affect my chances for promotion. Frankly, though, it didn't matter. It wasn't what was important at that moment.

"We dealt with more serious health issues for the next few years. During this time, I was indeed promoted. My supervisor at the time and one of my mentors, Major Mike Woods, shared with me something about his priorities that resonate with me to this day. He said that even though he is completely committed to our agency and his work every day, the job is about number-five on his priority list.

"I agree with his assessment and try to lead based on the idea that while I expect everyone to give one hundred percent every day, family and health are priority number one. I try to lead by example and encourage my employees to use their personal leave and sick time for what should be their priority: health and family."

As you can imagine, family is important to Lee. "As with anyone in our profession, there are times when family sacrifices have to be made. This is especially true of anyone who serves in a highly specialized unit such as aviation. Connor and Natalie are my two children, and I've missed a lot of their sporting events. I know it worries Angel when I get up in the middle of the night and rush out the door. Many times, I can't even tell her what I'm working on.

"I make every attempt to minimize the impact on my family. The kids don't know any different; it's what I've done all their lives. But law enforcement families are different—from the unpredictable schedule to the types of discussions you have with your wife and kids while watching the news or at the dinner table. They may not know it, but I think they're a little more prepared to handle adverse situations because of it."

For Those Outside Law Enforcement

I asked Lee if he had any thoughts he'd like to share with those outside the law enforcement profession. He said: "Most people in law enforcement are good, honest, hardworking folks just trying to earn a living and make a difference in their communities. We do this under the one-sided and often unfair watchful eye of news and social media outlets. We have to make split-second, life-and-death decisions that society will second-guess for days or years to come. Not everyone is built for or programmed to run toward gunfire. Be thankful for those in our society who are; they are your protectors."

Lee, thank you for your service to your community and being that eye and voice in the sky for your fellow first responders.

Sergeant Tina Haddon

Florida State University Police Department: Two Years
Tallahassee Police Department: Twenty-Three Years
Retired: Twenty-Five Years of Service

When Tina was hired at the Tallahassee Police Department (TPD), I was in my fifteenth year there and was the sergeant supervising our agency's Homicide Unit. Our paths crossed throughout our career, yet I never had the pleasure of working directly with her. Even so, I was able to watch her grow and her career blossom.

Tina is one of those individuals who knew early on in life that being a police officer was her chosen career path. As she told me, "Law enforcement is all I ever wanted to do. I remember being one of those kids in school who wore the orange sash as a member of the School Safety Patrol.

"In the fifth grade, I stood with the school crossing guard in front of the Woodville Elementary School on Highway 319 and helped kids cross the street. I joined the Explorers (a youth program) at the Leon County Sheriff's Office (LCSO) when I was fourteen and remained with them until I was nineteen or twenty. It was truly my calling, and I have known it as long as I can remember. No one in my immediate family is in law enforcement, so I have no idea why."

Tina shared her law enforcement journey with her best friend Kirk Watson. They met in the band room as freshman at Godby High School in Tallahassee. As Tina describes it, "We had this immediate connection. We just clicked as friends; there was never anything more to it. We joked about it - he was my brother from another mother.

"We both joined the Boy Scouts Explorer Program at the Leon County Sheriff's Office that same year. Kirk's father was a ranking officer at the time and retired as a major. Because of Mr. Watson's presence, we were more than Explorers. We basically hung out in the building all the time. We were there, in the band room at Godby High School or at my house or his. We were never ones to go out drinking or partying, but we were always together.

"We played board games with our parents and went bowling with our families. During our four years at Godby, we were in numerous classes together. Most of my memories from high school involved music classes. We were in the marching band, symphonic band, jazz band, and guitar classes together. I remember being mad at him in regular classes because he was so much smarter than me. He would sit and draw during class and not study for tests. He would make an A every time. I would take notes, pay attention, and study like crazy to make an A. Kirk was always one of the smartest people I knew.

"Upon graduation, we went to the Tallahassee Community College, and we were both members of the Marching Chiefs, the band at Florida State University (FSU). Kirk became a deputy at LCSO, and I finished my college degree. I rode with him often when he was a deputy."

Tina graduated from FSU in 1992, completed the police academy, and was hired as a police officer at the Florida State University Police Department (FSUPD) in 1993. She was hired by TPD as an officer in 1995.

Tina added, "Eventually, we were both hired by the Tallahassee Police Department (TPD). We answered calls together, caught bad guys together, and got awards together. If we were working the same shift, we almost always found a way to eat supper together or have a pint of ice cream as a snack. We loved to eat ice cream!

"Our friendship was like no other I have ever had. I truly see him as my brother. We spent holidays together. He taught me how to drive a stick shift, and I held his first child moments after she was born.

"During high school, we each met the person we would marry. Eventually, the four of us laughed, cried, played games, traveled, and generally lived life together. I could not have asked for two better friends than Kirk and his wife. I can't think of many things in my life that haven't included him in some way."

The Loss of a Best Friend

Tina and Kirk had the opportunity to work in several different areas at the police department. In 2005, Tina was assigned to the department's Training Unit, and Kirk was a K9 officer. Life circumstances changed, though; Kirk was diagnosed with colon cancer. He had surgery and endured chemotherapy but continued to work as much as possible and live life to the fullest. Tina said, "People had no idea of the commitment he made to stay alive. He loved being a K9 officer, and that was part of it, but his wife and children were the main reason he fought so hard.

"For nine years he fought. In 2015, Kirk died. I miss him so much, it hurts every day, and there are reminders everywhere I go. Kirk was a part of my life for more than thirty years, and there are times I don't know how I'm going to do something without him doing it with me. His wife is still very much a part of my life, and I love her like a sister. She got me by default when she found Kirk. We are still very much family."

Training Others: Her Favorite

A good portion of Tina's career has been centered on training. She was a field training officer (FTO), FTO sergeant, worked in TPD's training unit as a trainer, and eventually as the sergeant supervising the unit. It was no surprise that when I asked what her favorite position was, she told me FTO Sergeant and Citizens Police Academy Coordinator.

"I enjoyed these for different reasons. FTO Sergeant was challenging because I worked hard to train the FTOs and then watched them train the recruits. I thoroughly enjoyed seeing the recruits succeed and then the FTOs smile out of a sense of pride because they knew they had done a good job. That gave me a sense of pride because I helped them be better trainers. Ultimately, I felt I was able to make a difference two-fold because I helped both people. I loved seeing the success of others.

"With the Citizens Police Academy (CPA), I loved interacting with citizens, building a bond, and teaching about law enforcement. It was a phenomenal experience. I run into people all the time who completed the CPA while I was the coordinator, and they all smile and tell me about something they experienced during the program. But it gave me more than that; it gave me some cherished friendships.

"Two particular individuals ended up being mentors to me, teaching me so much about life. Sadly, both of those individuals died in 2015, the same year as Kirk. I still talk on a regular basis with the wife of one of my mentors; she is the picture of strength. I love the friendships I made, cherish the time I had with everyone, and grieve the losses."

Training the Trainer

Police officers in most departments are required to attend annual training/qualifications. Many of the topics are mandated by law, such as firearms qualification and use of force among others. Time is often allotted for other related topics, and I'm happy to see that some of these topics are more personal in nature.

Over the past few years, these have included how to deal with the physical stress of the job and the importance of proper nutrition. Imagine wearing an additional thirty pounds of gear around your waist every day for the life of your career. It takes its toll on your neck, back, and hips. I'm living proof of that. I'm proud of TPD for providing training on these topics.

Tina told me that as a follow-up to these topics, this year they are focusing on mental health. This is often ignored or less talked-about, not just for law enforcement officers but for all first responders. However, that is changing.

She said, "This year we're doing a class called 'Understanding Law Enforcement Induced Stress,' which focuses on mental health. The class is intended to be a discussion about the different types of stress, the signs and symptoms of stress, and formal and informal resources to help with stress.

"We talk about two main types—cumulative stress and the singular event type of stress. These singular events, or calls for service, can be a part of the cumulative stress. I contacted retirees who I knew had experience helping people, most with formalized training, and all who had a critical incident or cumulative stress they were willing to share to help others. There are seven of us who facilitate the classes.

Dealing with Job Stress

"I decided to do this because, like everyone who does this job, I've experienced the stress over the course of a long career, and I've seen how it affects other people. I had to learn coping skills to deal with the stress of the various types of things we see as police officers. As the training sergeant, I wanted to go further and talk about the deep, dark secret of risky behaviors related to stress, such as drinking, drugs, divorce, and suicide in law enforcement.

"In 2017, more officers died from suicide than were killed in the line of duty. People are willing to help with healthy ways of dealing with stress. It's important that we start the conversation in the hope that officers will feel more comfortable reaching out for help when they need it. There is such a stigma of asking for help within the law enforcement profession.

"We see and experience things most citizens don't, and we must take a proactive role in teaching officers that their reactions to calls are normal and that seeking help is okay. So many say they get into law enforcement to help people but then forget to help each other. I'm hoping that through this discussion, officers will not only be willing to seek help but be willing to start a conversation with an officer who might need help."

When I asked Tina to tell me what the most difficult part of her job was, it mirrored her thoughts about stress. "I have physical scars from doing the job, but I also have emotional scars. I can't go to very many places in Tallahassee without remembering a call for service and thinking about someone who died there, how I worked a traffic homicide there, how I worked an officer-involved shooting there, or how I got into a fight there. Even off duty, I recall so much.

"I say all of that to give perspective to my most difficult part of the job: the people who accuse me of being racist when I step out of my patrol car. They don't know me and don't know what

I have given to my community and agency. But because I'm a police officer, I'm judged before I even speak.

"If I judge citizens by their clothes, skin color, or other factors, I could be disciplined by my agency because those people can file a complaint against me. Often, citizens have no accountability. They can say anything they want about me, write articles and publish them, post on social media sites, or just incite a crowd on a scene. I must just take it. I've learned to do that, but for me, that is by far the worst part of this job.

"I want to be seen for who I am, what I stand for, and the job I do. I want to be given the chance to serve the citizens fully. Complain if I do a bad job, but don't judge me by the uniform I wear and the car I drive. Citizens don't want policing decisions to be made on external factors; they don't want to be judged based on them, and neither do I. Citizens want to be treated fairly for who they are or what they've done. So, do I."

Seeing the Victims as People

I followed this up by asking Tina if she had what most would call a career-defining moment. She said, "In 1998, I was dispatched to a call where a suspect had forced his way into an apartment and sexually battered several roommates and shot at least one, maybe two. It was a brutal scene. I was one of the first officers there. A strange fact—there were four female victims, and the first five officers to arrive on the scene were all female.

"We closed the scene because each victim had an officer with her, and the fifth controlled the access. Our sergeant was female. The lead forensic technician was female. The homicide sergeant was female. None of that was planned, but to me, that was awesome. I don't often think about being a 'female' cop. I just do my job. On this day, though, it was phenomenal to be a part of the response as all females!

"I ended up with a victim who had been shot after being sexually battered. Her brother was in town, but her parents lived in Central Florida. I rode in the ambulance with her, and then while they provided medical care in the emergency room, I held her hand. I stayed with her for hours until her brother was located and arrived. She was in a lot of pain emotionally and physically, and I was there for her.

"Once her brother showed up, I joined the hunt for the suspect. The next day, my squad walked door to door seeking information. I was hurting so bad from being on my feet for hours, but I was invested in the outcome. Several hours into the shift, our homicide investigators and forensic technicians not only identified the suspect, but TAC (our agency's name for our SWAT team) chased him down and arrested him.

"The homicide sergeant, Donna Brown, allowed me to go to the hospital and tell the victim and her parents that the suspect was in custody. There has never been another moment in my career like that. The outward sigh of relief from her parents was overwhelming.

"Several months later, I received a thank-you letter from the victim's mother. I also saw them in our forensics unit not long after she got out of the hospital. I saw the victim in a totally different light, and it was a closure of sorts for me. As patrol officers, we rarely get to see our victims outside the initial call for service. I have never forgotten her name or the specific details of those twenty-four hours in my career."

A Newfound Passion

Every law enforcement agency has a plan for natural disasters, especially those in Florida. Unlike other disasters, you can prepare for hurricanes. Tina found a second calling in this area. "When Hurricane Katrina made landfall in 2005, I had the honor of deploying to Mississippi on a law enforcement response team. We answered calls for service in Hancock County, Mississippi.

"I was with all TPD officers. We slept in a tent for two weeks, cooked and ate as a group, and patrolled the county during the day. As tragic as it was, the experience was like no other. Another team from the city of Tallahassee deployed as an Incident Management Team, and they deployed to a different county and managed that county's resources for them. I didn't see them work, but I heard about their work. I saw the same work being done in our county by another team. I found my passion.

"When we returned home, someone I considered my mentor gave me a chance on the city's Emergency Management Team, and I was hooked. I played minor roles for a couple of years but got the chance to be the Planning Section Chief. I was very excited.

"Not long after I got that position, the city and county co-located to our then new Public Safety Complex. The county didn't have a Plans Section, so the city's Plans Section filled the role until just recently. I have guided the group through several twelve-hour activations and two nine-day activations. The nine-day activations were for Hurricanes Irma and Hermine.

"For those two hurricanes, I worked fourteen- to sixteen-hour days for nine days straight. A few of those days, I didn't even go home; I just napped in the building and went right back to work. The Plans Section documents everything that happens, so if we can apply for FEMA assistance, we have the proper documentation to support our claim. It was tedious work, but I loved it.

"TPD has a couple of roles in the Emergency Operations Center (EOC). We staff the Police Liaison Desk. The police department has a representative at the desk, and they work as the direct link between the police department and the EOC. We also serve in other roles based on training, experience, and desire to do the work. TPD currently holds the positions of Plans Section Chief (city and county) and Operations Section Chief (city). This is also due to training, experience, and desire.

"That said, I'm honored to have served as the Plans Section Chief for Tallahassee/Leon County. I have learned so much and have been able to work with great people.

A big stress for me during EOC activations, though, is my family. "Like everyone else who works these events, we are away from our families for days at a time. Our power goes out. We have trees down and damage to our homes. But to get the ball rolling in the right direction for the community as a whole, someone must coordinate the response effort, and I chose to be a part of it.

"At times like this, most first responders work night and day while their families are on their own having to repair damaged homes and keep the generators going. Many people in the community are given administrative days off from work by their employers in times like this. Not first responders or EOC staff. Our families must do it without us. I enjoyed the work, but it always came with guilt."

Tina has taken her newfound passion and desire to be involved to a higher level and explained, "I have received certification through the state of Florida as a Plans Section Chief. This took a lot of training and real-world work. This certification allows me to be deployed to other jurisdictions to help coordinate a response to various types of incidents or events. I am extremely proud of this certification as it was not easy to obtain. I know others who applied but were denied, so I hold it with much respect. I am deeply thankful to those who helped me along the way; this is not something you do alone."

This was not the only certification she has obtained. "I am also a Master Exercise Practitioner (MEP). This is an extensive training program through FEMA/Department of Homeland Security (DHS) to certify someone to design and conduct training exercises. This helps to ensure we are all being consistent in our training, establishes a framework we all strive toward, and can open a path to various grants based on the gaps identified during the exercise. This training had numerous prerequisites that I completed in Florida but finished with four weeks at the Emergency Management Institute (EMI) in Emmitsburg, Maryland. Again, I must thank those who helped me achieve this certification; it, too, isn't completed alone."

Going Above and Beyond

With all that Tina has accomplished and has been involved with, I asked her to tell me what she felt was the most rewarding part of her job as a police officer. She said, "By far, the most rewarding part has been the relationships I have built over the years. I've touched on some of those, but the most important one is that I met my wife of twenty years at TPD. I also met one of my best friends at the Florida State University Police Department (FSUPD) in 1993.

"But it's also the everyday calls for service that mean so much. That old cliché of the reason why we all became cops was to 'help someone' is truly the most rewarding part. I responded to a young man's house that had been burglarized. He was a newly licensed barber, and the burglar stole his clippers. He was devastated and unable to afford new ones. I was able to buy him a new pair, and his smile was so worth it.

"I used to love sitting and talking with two particular homeless men because they had done and seen things I will never get to do or see. I loved giving police stickers to kids. It used to bother me when parents would threaten their kids with, 'If you don't behave, that police officer is going to take you to jail.' We don't want kids to be afraid of police officers, so I'd talk to the kids and give them a junior police badge sticker.

"Several years ago, I got together with a few of my squad mates, and we paid the electricity bill for a family who was struggling. They were so thankful for the gift. Officers everywhere do things like this every day. I get smiles and hugs, and I go home happy knowing that at least on that day, a police officer wasn't judged by his/her uniform or car but by the person he/she is."

The Support of Family

Most police officers know the sacrifices their families make because of their jobs. They also know they couldn't do their job without their support. It's the same with Tina. "My mother has supported me from day one. She was the one who drove me to the Explorer events before I could drive. She has been at all my graduations, swearing-in ceremonies, awards ceremonies, and my promotion. She lived the life with me by arranging holiday events and birthday suppers around my schedule for twenty-five years. Never has she complained and has always been willing to help if I needed it.

"My sister Michelle has been wonderful too. She lives close, has ridden with me on patrol several times, and listens when I need it. I love that she and her husband live close by, and we can do everyday life things together. My mother and sister went through the Citizen's Police Academy when I was the coordinator to learn more about my career.

"As a police officer, my best friend/"brother" Kirk had the same crazy lifestyle and schedule. That made it easy for our families to enjoy holidays together. Rarely did we celebrate a holiday on the actual day, but we always celebrated together, and we all knew that was the most important part.

"Family and friends are so important to me, but at the top of my list is my wife, whom I first met when we were in high school.

She was a little older than me and was hired at TPD before me, and our paths crossed early in my career. Sheri was an amazing trainer who helped me tremendously through the FTO program. We developed a great friendship, and as time went on, we fell in love and eventually married. We've been together over twenty years. She retired after twenty-five years of combined service in the United States Army and TPD. We look forward to a long life together and enjoying our retirement. Sheri is my hero, my mentor, my best friend, my partner, and my everything. I cannot imagine my life without her.

"My family has been there for me through good times and bad, illnesses and injuries. All of them helped me get to where I am in life. I'm thankful for the time I have had with some and memories still to come with others."

Find an Identity Outside of Your Work

I always ask everyone if they have any personal thoughts they'd like to pass along. Tina said, "To those who don't work in law enforcement, please remember we're not 'what' we do. We are real people who have families, hobbies, power outages for days due to hurricanes, grieve when our brother and friends die, and celebrate milestones and holidays just like our fellow citizens. We are people. We are not the uniform or the badge. We have chosen a difficult and noble profession and take pride in the work we do.

"To those who still wear the uniform, thank you for your service. Keep your head held high, and do work you're proud of, but find an identity other than 'the work you do.'"

I try to attend as many retirement ceremonies as I can, and I was fortunate to make Tina's. One of TPD's traditions is to give the retiring officer their duty weapon, and Tina received hers. But she was also given something very special: the shotgun that had been issued to Kirk. A small plaque was placed on it with his name and badge number and two superhero logos, a passion Kirk and Tina shared. Kirk's mother and father were there for the presentation, a very special moment.

If the number of people in attendance and the many different agencies represented is any indication of the impact that Tina had throughout her career, it was huge. Thank you for your service, Tina, and enjoy Phase 2 of your life. You've earned it.

Captain Rory Robbins

**Florida State University Police Department:
One Year
Leon County Sheriff's Office: Twenty-Nine Years
Retired: Thirty Years of Service**

Rory and I met several years ago in an unusual way. We each were working in law enforcement. I was with the Tallahassee Police Department, and Rory was with our sister agency, the Leon County Sheriff's Office. He's a humble man and consummate professional; it was a pleasure to watch his career progress. For these and several other reasons, Rory was an easy choice for this book.

I ask everyone how they came to be a law enforcement officer, and Rory said, "I considered a career in law enforcement while still in high school. I was interested in both the Florida Highway Patrol and the Florida Wildlife Commission; however, I chose to go to college after high school. Growing up in Live Oak, Florida, I worked on a large farm all through high school and into junior college. I also worked for my dad at his service station while in junior college. I give my parents credit for the morals they instilled in me and specifically, my dad for helping to develop my work ethic because our station was a true 'service station.' We checked under the hood, checked the tires, washed the windshield, and pumped the gas for the customers. Dad always told me 'If a job's worth doing, it's worth doing right.'"

Rory attended North Florida Junior College where he met his wife Kayla; they had two classes together. Kayla's father was a career Florida Highway Patrol trooper, and on their first date, she told Rory that she would never marry a cop. Love won out, and Rory said, "I didn't pursue a career in law enforcement."

When Rory graduated in 1984, he moved to Tallahassee to be closer to Kayla, who was now attending Florida State University. They married in 1985.

Florida State University Police Department

Instead of finishing his education, he entered the workforce, but nothing was fulfilling or offered a career path. A friend of his mentioned that the FSU Police Department was hiring. He talked to Kayla about it, applied, and was hired in 1987; Kayla was now married to a cop!

Rory said, "Attending the police academy is where my passion really began for my new career." The FSUPD is a small agency, and for Rory, a good place to begin. He enjoyed working there. Later that year, a friend he met in the academy called to let him know that the Leon County Sheriff's Office was hiring. Rory told him that he was happy and didn't have plans to leave.

A few months later, his friend called again and encouraged Rory to come talk with his shift lieutenant. Rory agreed to meet with the lieutenant. "I went from having no intention of leaving FSUPD to completing an application, having a formal interview, and being fitted for uniforms in less than twenty-four hours."

It was an adjustment for Rory. He went from patrolling a large college campus to patrolling on his own where his nearest backup officer was often several minutes away. "I had to grow up pretty fast; the types of calls I was responding to and the pace of the work was very different."

School Resource Officer with the Leon County Sheriff's Office

In 1989, Rory became a school resource officer and was placed in one of the larger high schools in the county. School resource officers (SROs) are often a topic of discussion with school safety being a high priority. With Rory's experience as a school resource officer and in supervising LCSO's unit at the sergeant, lieutenant, and captain levels, I asked him to explain in greater detail about school resource officers.

At that time, the only specific training required was the completion of a forty-hour basic school resource officer class. LCSO's unit consisted of fourteen SROs, one sergeant, and one lieutenant, and was one of the first agencies in the state of Florida to incorporate SROs into the school system. When Rory retired, the unit had grown to twenty-four SROs, two sergeants, one lieutenant, and one captain.

He went into further detail. "The philosophy behind the program is multi-faceted, to obviously provide security and presence on the campus, but to also educate through personal interaction and teaching various programs in the classroom, whenever possible. It's also, to investigate crimes on campus, enforce the law, work runaway cases, and provide counseling to students. One of the main reasons to be on campus is to break down barriers between law enforcement and civilians, hoping to form positive relationships between the two, build trust, and to truly let the students see there is a normal person beyond the badge.

"Other duties of the SRO consist of providing security for school functions such as football and basketball games, and whatever the school feels a need for extra security. I have always said the SROs consistently work more scheduled hours than any other unit in the agency. SROs rotate being on call for a week at a time. Duties for the on-call SRO would include working runaway cases, large underage drinking parties, school threat assessments, or anything else deemed necessary by the supervisors.

"Many people think SROs have the summer off as well as all the school holidays. There is some truth to that but not nearly as much as people think. The SROs are rarely granted personal leave while school is in session. For this reason, the occasional teacher workday or school holiday is a welcomed sight. They are pretty much on campus from thirty minutes before school starts to thirty minutes after school releases for the day, and most eat lunch on campus every day. Even though school may be out, depending on the number of days and the supervisor's discretion, at least the on-call SRO has to work, and often at least one or two others, in case of an emergency, especially over long breaks like Christmas, spring break, and Thanksgiving.

"The summer is when most SROs try to take vacation; however, they have to fit it in between various activities that only the SROs work. For LCSO, those activities included two weeks of local youth camps, serving approximately thirty kids each week. We also attended a dozen sessions of a teen-driving program, which were two days each, serving an average of ten students each session. SROs also volunteered to work a week at either the Florida Sheriff's Boys Ranch or the Carruth Youth Camp.

"Summer is the time when most SROs attended the annual weeklong SRO conference, which consists of various training sessions and interaction with SROs from other agencies. In addition, they spend about a week updating their mandatory agency training prior to school starting back. Some SROs also assisted other units within the department with special events or with other units that might be experiencing a staffing shortage. As you can see, there really isn't much down time for school resource officers.

"LCSO began requiring SROs to attend the forty-hour basic SRO school and eighty-hour Instructor Techniques class. They also, along with the rest of the agency, are required to train in active-shooter response. SROs are encouraged to attend advanced training as often as possible. As I progressed in rank, I attended many other training classes that were related to the SRO position and unit."

Campus Crime

I asked Rory if he could describe the types of things he did or encountered as an SRO, and he provided these scenarios: "I've broken up many fights between students, dealt with students who attacked teachers or school staff, and others who were suspended and refused to leave campus. The campus of the high school where I worked was an open campus; there was no fence around the school.

"This allowed easy access to the campus for those who were not students and shouldn't have been on the property. The staff and students were aware of this, and at times were my extra eyes and ears. I recall one incident.

"Classes were in session, and I was walking around the campus. I encountered a teenage boy I didn't recognize as a student. My high school had approximately eighteen hundred students at the time. I didn't know them all, but I knew the vast majority by face. As I approached the teenager, I noticed his pockets were bulging more than normal.

"I confronted him and confirmed he wasn't a student and had no business being on campus. As I started to pat him down, he resisted and tried to reach for his back pocket. Fearing he had a weapon, I pinned him to a car and radioed for help. He continued to struggle and try to reach his pocket.

"A staff member arrived to help, and we were able to take him into custody. After searching him, I found a knife and a screwdriver in the pocket he was reaching for. He also had a large amount of change in his pockets. We suspected he had just broken into the drink machine in the gym, which we had been having problems with. We checked those machines, and they were intact.

"Ultimately, it was discovered that the subject had just committed an armed burglary to a home next to campus. The teenager had broken into the home while an elderly woman was sleeping in the same room he stole the money from, and he armed himself with the knife."

Rory told me that of all the different positions he served in, being an SRO was his favorite and explained further, "I tried to learn the names of as many of the students as I could, and I tried to build relationships and trust between us. I would make an effort to call them by name whenever I saw them because I wanted them to know that they mattered to me.

"Probably the most important thing I learned from being in the school is how good most of the kids are. Working on the road, often juvenile calls were very difficult for one reason or another. Being in the school, I really got to know a lot of them. I often was able to understand what was going on with them when they made a poor decision and help them through it. The most advantageous thing was to be able to follow up with a student on a regular basis. On patrol, that was rare.

"Being only twenty-six years old when I started at the school, I wasn't too much older than many of the students. They loved to call me by my first name, which I didn't mind; I have never been a stickler about titles. It was all about treating them with respect and getting that respect in return. I learned early on that kids took everything you said literally. It was, and is, important to be honest and consistent with them.

"I developed several friendships with students that have continued over the years. Probably the most satisfying result from working as an SRO is the relationships made and the impact you have on a young person. I still have people come up to me and say they remember me being their SRO. Even kids who I had small issues with come up to me and say what a positive impact I had on them. They got their lives in order and are happy. Those interactions mean the most. That is the most rewarding thing an SRO can experience.

Criminal Investigation Bureau Detective

Rory left the School Resource Officer Unit and transferred to the Criminal Investigation Bureau as a detective. He also became a member of the department's SWAT team. During this time, Rory decided to go back to school and complete his college degree.

That's how Rory and I met. For many years our agency, the Tallahassee Police Department (TPD), and the Leon County Sheriff's Office (LCSO) had a joint Robbery Task Force. It was comprised of four investigators and detectives, two from TPD and two from LCSO. It alternated being housed at the police department and at the sheriff's office.

In 1996, I was supervising the Homicide Unit at TPD. My division commander told me that the Robbery Task Force was physically moving back to TPD headquarters in its own office on the same floor as all the other investigative units – just down the hall from my office where I would be supervising the unit. Rory was a member of the task force.

Part of Rory's graduation requirements was to complete a semester-long internship. We were able to help out. Rory added, "I want to give a special thanks to the folks at TPD for letting me intern there while working in the Robbery Task Force."

Supervising both units was at times a challenge due to the volume of work the two units handled. But Rory, the other detective from LCSO, and our two investigators from TPD were professional and hard-working, and it was a pleasure to work with each of them.

Rory proudly told me, "In 1997, I graduated from Florida State University and fulfilled my promise to my parents and walked at the graduation ceremony. It was very difficult going back to school while carrying a caseload as a detective and trying to be an involved father to two young girls.

"I could have completed some of my coursework online, but I wanted to be in the classroom to really understand it. With the help of my supervisors, allowing me at times to alter my schedule, it took going to class at night, on my lunch hour, in the morning, and stacking classes during the summer to graduate. But I did it."

Violent Crimes Unit

In December 1997, Rory was transferred back to LCSO and became a member of the Violent Crimes Unit as a detective. He was promoted to sergeant in 1998, to lieutenant in 2005, and to captain in 2014. He supervised a multitude of units including a Field Training Squad, several investigative units, the Crime Prevention Unit, and spent seven years with the School Resource Officer Unit, to mention a few.

As for the most difficult part of his job, he explained, "The most difficult part of my job was delivering death notifications, especially informing parents that their child had been killed in a car crash. It's so unexpected and tragic. As a school resource officer, it was working runaways. Some were chronic, and some just didn't get along with their parents, but some of these kids were troubled. One young girl I remember; in my heart I knew she was one of those with deeper issues. I couldn't get to the root of the problem, why she was constantly running away. I always felt she was hiding something. There was a positive ending though; I ran into her years later as an adult, and she was leading a productive life.

"The one that really haunts me is a young boy who ran away. We did everything we could possibly do and sadly, he has never been seen or heard from again. Cases like that can haunt you because you feel like you failed or just didn't do enough."

I also asked Rory if he had what he might consider a "career-defining moment." He told me, "I have no one career-defining moment; I have had several little things throughout my career that helped to confirm in my mind that I chose the right profession. The fact that former students still recognize me and call me by name, twenty-five plus years later, makes me smile. Some even keep in contact with me. For me, it makes me feel that I did something right.

"Having those I arrested thank me for treating them with respect or come up to me many years later in a restaurant, shake my hand, and thank me for what I did for them is priceless.

"One thing that was unexpected in my career happened in 1996. I was asked to transfer to the Robbery Task Force. I was a burglary detective and had young kids at home and took classes at FSU. I knew in my mind that if I didn't finish school this time, I never would, and I really wanted to finish.

Robbery Task Force

"Everything I knew about the Robbery Task Force was that you were on call a tremendous amount of the time, and you got called out a lot. I didn't think I would be able to keep up in school with that kind of schedule. I initially declined the offer but realized career-wise it was best if I accepted it. So I agreed to go. My office would be at the Tallahassee Police Department, a totally new environment.

"The task force was as busy as I had always heard, but there were some shining lights waiting on me. I was welcomed with open arms and treated well. To top it off, I had a fantastic supervisor, Sergeant Donna Brown. As it turned out, I faced one of the positions I feared most to work, and it turned out to be one of the best assignments of my career. I gained a tremendous amount of experience, made a lot of new friends and colleagues, and I believe it ultimately contributed to future promotions. Not to mention, I got to witness a bank robbery attempt go down on a stakeout, which most people don't get to experience."

Rory was always active with charitable causes while working at LCSO, but knowing him as I do, his faith and his family have always been his priority. He currently serves on his church's staff, Parish Relations Committee, and with the Men's Ministry Group.

This was important to him to have included in his story: "Even though she was initially against me going into law enforcement, Kayla has been my biggest supporter from day one. Whenever times got tough for me, I could always rely on her support at the end of the day.

"It was difficult for her at times, like other spouses, when we all would go out to work during a hurricane or a SWAT callout, not knowing when we would come home. But she managed well. And during those years, she gave me three beautiful and wonderful children.

"In 1994, Alexis, my oldest child, was three years old when my daughter Sydney was born. At the time, I was a burglary detective, fairly new on the SWAT team, and attending classes every semester at FSU to complete my degree. I was stretched thin. She was so supportive and held down the home fort while I was so busy with all those other things.

"When my third child, Kyle, was born in 1998, I had graduated from college and was at a point to where we could afford for Kayla to stay home and focus on raising the kids. The kids are now all grown, and I believe we have been truly blessed. They have followed somewhat in our footsteps as being servants to others. Alexis is a kindergarten teacher, her husband Alex is a police officer, Sydney is a registered nurse, and Kyle is a United States Marine. Kayla has since gone back to work in the school system.

"I can't complain about missing too many functions because of work. I did miss some, but timing was often good for me, and many of my supervisors were family-oriented and helped me and others work around special occasions whenever possible. I was always active, but a knee injury made me realize it was time to retire from playing sports and focus on the next chapter with my kids.

"I was very active with my children growing up. They all were involved in activities starting at an early age. Sports were always an important part of my life growing up, so I wanted my kids to experience that as well. They played soccer, t-ball, softball, baseball, flag football, and golf and they danced, I helped coach as much as I could and attended as much as possible. I know God comes first, but my family is a very close second. They are who define me."

<u>Understanding the Life of a Cop</u>

I asked Rory if he had any thoughts that he'd like to share. "I would like to pass onto the civilian world to not let the actions of a few make you think all cops are bad or out to get you. As in all walks of life, there are good people and some bad ones. There are some people who don't belong in law enforcement. For whatever reason, they are not cut out for it, or their ego is too big, or they get into it for the wrong reasons. It's often hard to identify these at the beginning of their career.

"We try hard to select good people, and most are. The vast majority of us really have your best interest at heart. We all live in the same community and want it to be safe for our families and yours.

"The next time you see an officer parked somewhere or sitting alone, take a step back and try to give him the benefit of the doubt. He may have just left a call for service where he had to work something horrific, perhaps a death investigation, an elder abuse case, a child abuse case, or perform CPR, just to name a few possibilities. That officer has to relive the whole call after the fact by writing the report. He can't go home just because he had to deal with something terrible; he must finish his shift and be there for the next call.

"Sometimes there just isn't any time to decompress, so officers may come to your minor traffic crash right after one of those bad calls. Or they may just be having a welcomed slow day, but they are always on call at a moment's notice to handle the next call. I'm not trying to make excuses because there is no excuse for rudeness or lack of doing your job, but I'm just trying to help you understand what might be going on in the officer's mind.

"They usually won't share those things and certainly can't with you. We are people too. Those bad things affect us, but we often must wear a mask to cover our feelings so the general public won't see what's going on inside. So please, just say a little prayer for them when you see officers or think about them."

Rory, thank you for your service! Keep enjoying your retirement. You earned it.

Tonja Bryant-Smith

Special Agent Supervisor
Tallahassee Police Department: Eleven Years
Florida Department of Law Enforcement: Sixteen Years
Active Duty: Twenty-Seven Years of Service

Tonja laughingly told me that her main reason for entering law enforcement was "Because I wanted to be a plain clothes detective like Tubbs on the television show *Miami Vice*. I truly felt that being a police officer, I could make a difference."

Tonja graduated from Florida State University (FSU) in 1991 with a bachelor of science degree in criminology. Later that year, she was hired by the Tallahassee Police Department (TPD) and completed the police academy in February 1992.

She spent her first five years as a patrol officer answering service calls. In her sixth year, Tonja was transferred and served as a Crime Prevention Officer and Community Relations Officer.

For Tonja, "My favorite position was serving as a Crime Prevention Officer. It really helped to develop me as an officer, certainly enhanced my public speaking skills, but also helped build a great, positive bridge with the community. This position was all about the community, and that's where I truly felt I was able to help and make a difference. I loved all of the positive interactions it afforded me with the Officer Friendly Program, neighborhood watch group meetings, and safety awareness presentations."

The Florida Department of Law Enforcement

In 2002, Tonja left TPD and was hired by the Florida Department of Law Enforcement (FDLE) as a special agent. FDLE is a state agency with 1,890 employees; five hundred twenty-two of those employees are sworn law enforcement officers.

I asked Tonja why she chose to leave TPD. "It really wasn't something that was a part of my career path. I was working at a recruitment fair representing TPD and met an FDLE agent. FDLE was a much larger agency, and I felt it could afford me a greater chance of experiencing a variety of positions. There was the opportunity to conduct short-term and long-term investigations in a non-uniform role. I took a chance and applied."

Tonja was hired not knowing exactly what unit she would be working with. On her first day with FDLE, she was told that she was being assigned to the narcotics unit. She explained, "This was a new area for me, and I knew very little about the narcotics aspect of law enforcement. FDLE sent me to basic and advanced training with the United States Drug Enforcement Administration (DEA), and I got a lot of on-the-job training. FDLE even bought me fake gold teeth and different wigs so that I could change my appearance." Tonja spent five years as an undercover narcotics agent.

During her time in this role, Tonja earned her first promotion to Inspector and was assigned to the Professional Standards/Internal Affairs Unit. This unit also investigated and reviewed allegations of misconduct and violations involving FDLE members. Tonja explained that this was one of her more challenging assignments. "We investigated members who were law enforcement officers and others who held positions of public trust. It was difficult and stressful having to arrest some of your own but crucial to maintaining the trust and faith of the community."

Tonja remained in this unit for four years. During those years, there were times when she served as the Acting Supervisor. She felt she was ready for the next step and applied to become a Special Agent Supervisor. The promotional process is not an easy one with FDLE. Tonja said, "Our process consists of taking a written test. Once you pass the test, you participate in a Supervisor Assessment Process, which includes an inbox exercise, a public speaking presentation, and then an oral board. You apply for openings in whichever office currently has one, and there can be an additional oral board. The last step is an interview with the commissioner who has the final decision."

Specialty Units

She was promoted and assigned to the Counterterrorism Unit in the Tallahassee Regional Operations Center (TROC). "The main purpose of this unit is to deal with threats, sovereign citizens, and domestic and international security issues. I'm also the Mutual Aid Coordinator and responsible for the Regional Domestic Security Task Force and the North Florida Fusion Exchange. We also have two Federal Bureau of Investigation (FBI) Joint Terrorism Task Force agents, four FDLE agents, two crime intelligence analysts, and a domestic security planner. In addition, we have a telecommunications consultant who oversees regional assets such as the storm/hurricane trailers, command vehicles, and other specialized assets."

FDLE is broken into seven regions, and in the Tallahassee region, there are thirteen counties. Tonja said, "We also have smaller field offices in some of the larger regions. Tallahassee has a field office in Live Oak, Florida, which handles six of the thirteen counties, and the Tallahassee main office handles the other seven counties. Even though we are responsible for the thirteen counties in our region, FDLE has statewide jurisdiction. We work a lot with local, state, and federal agencies. Most of our investigations are joint investigations with other agencies, and we are an added resource for them. This can be additional personnel, financial assistance for narcotics investigations, and enhanced computer skills. We also assist in locating suspects in other areas of the state."

Those, such as Tonja, who are assigned to specialty units often find themselves on call as part of their duties. I asked Tonja to describe what that entails for her. "As a supervisor, I'm on call for the thirteen counties in our region every six weeks. But because I'm a Counterterrorism Supervisor, I am, for the most part, on call all of the time. My call week starts on a Friday and runs until the following Thursday at midnight. We're called out for a variety of issues including all life-threatening injuries or deaths within the Florida Department of Corrections prisons."

Tonja explained what that means for her and other FDLE agents during hurricane season. "As the Mutual Aid Coordinator for our region, I'm involved with any natural disaster that occurs. I've been deployed to various hurricanes during my time at FDLE. Part of my duties are staffing the Emergency Operation Centers for our thirteen counties. This includes deploying assets to the affected areas and tracking those resources. FDLE, as a whole, plays a major role as first responders in natural disasters for the entire state of Florida, but we have also responded to assist areas outside the state."

Stressors and Rewards

I asked Tonja what she would consider the most difficult part of her job. "I would have to say that my time as an undercover narcotics officer was one of the more stressful positions I've had. Most of the targets we dealt with had extensive criminal backgrounds, so safety was a high priority, not just for us, but if we utilized a confidential informant, their safety as well. Often, these are stressful situations, and we had to trust that our coworkers and officers from other agencies had our back."

While the job has its stresses and difficult times, it also has its rewards. Tonja said, "The most rewarding part of the job for me is the love and support I've received from TPD and FDLE. I still work a lot with TPD in my current position, and the people at both agencies will always be family. I do a lot of community service, which helps me foster positive relationships both inside and outside of my agency. I travel all over the state and sometimes to other states doing presentations that benefit children and adults. The children are our future. I've been afforded so many opportunities during my career, and for this I am grateful."

When I asked Tonja if she had a career-defining moment, she responded, "I've had a few different ones I could consider career-defining, but one stands out for me. It was a totally new mindset for me when I left TPD and began working at FDLE as a narcotics officer. On one occasion, I recall dropping off a confidential informant at a location, and not long after that, getting a really bad feeling that something wasn't right.

"I called and had a marked patrol car drive through the area intentionally so that our suspect, our target, would leave the area. Just as I was arriving to pick up my informant, three males showed up. My gut told me that they would have attacked my informant had I not come back to the area to pick them up. It's that sixth sense that people often describe and officers routinely rely on. It was a powerful reminder to trust mine."

While Tonja stays busy in her current position with FDLE, she's also actively involved with the National Organization of Black Law Enforcement Executives (NOBLE). She explained, "The mission of NOBLE is to ensure equity in the administration of justice in the provision of public service to all communities. It's also to serve as the conscience of law enforcement by being committed to justice by action. The goal of NOBLE is to be recognized as a highly competent public service organization that's at the forefront of providing solutions to both law enforcement issues and concerns as well as to our communities ever-changing needs.

"Our North Florida chapter has over fifty members who are from local, state, and federal agencies. We encourage positive relationships between law enforcement and the community. Some of the activities we participate in are holiday-related, such as the Christmas toy drive and putting together Thanksgiving baskets. But we also do things for the elder population in our community and for the kids preparing to head back to school for a new year.

"I have had the honor and privilege to be the president for our chapter for the past four years. I was recently selected as the national 2018 NOBLE member of the year. NOBLE has over sixty chapters and three thousand members. This award is the highest for our organization. It was a huge honor for me." Tonja is also a proud member of the Delta Sigma Theta sorority, Inc.

Tonja is married and has one son. He's twenty-three years old and a graduate student at James Madison University in Harrisonburg, Virginia. Her parents are an active support system for her and her family, and she has a brother and two nieces whom she truly adores. "I'm a very family-oriented person, and they are a huge part of my life."

When asked if she had any other thoughts she wanted to pass on, she shared, "Don't let anyone tell you that you can't do something. When I graduated from college, I had people tell me that I couldn't be a cop. Friends told me that I was too 'cute' to be a cop, as most female cops are 'manly looking.' Stereotypes. As I look back, those who made those comments to me are no longer a part of my life. Have a strong support system in place. My family has always supported me no matter what, one hundred percent."

Thank you, Tonja, for your service to your community.

THE VILLAGE OF FIRST RESPONDERS

Betty Green

Mother of Tallahassee Police Department Sergeant Dale Green, Killed in the Line of Duty November 13, 2002

Family is important to law enforcement officers and to all first responders. They realize their shift work and missing holidays and family functions can bring hardships. They also know in their hearts that with each parting kiss or hug, it could be their last. The families know this, too.

In the Volume I of *Behind and Beyond the Badge,* I included a story about Nicole Romans Hall, the wife of Police Sergeant Ervin Romans II, who had been killed in the line of duty. I think it's important that these stories be told because they're part of what is behind and beyond each badge. I wanted another such story for this book and instantly thought of Mrs. Green. So, in the early stages of planning this book, I reached out to her and told her about the first book, and that I was working on Volume II.

Spouses of those killed in the line of duty are at the forefront when tragedy strikes, and often the parents remain in the shadows. I seek to change this by including her thoughts about losing her son in the line of duty, from a mother's perspective. In some small way, I felt it would be an opportunity to honor Dale. Mrs. Green kindly agreed to let me tell her story.

There's Been an Accident

In 2002, I was the detective sergeant supervising the Tallahassee Police Department's Homicide Unit. Our unit was also responsible for investigating assaults on police officers. This included responding to and working the crime scene, coordinating efforts among various units, conducting interviews of witnesses and suspects, preparing the case file for the State Attorney's Office for the prosecution of suspects, and attending autopsies.

On the night Sergeant Dale Green was killed, I was called at home, told that he had been shot, and informed that I was to respond to the crime scene. I met Mrs. Green the following day.

She said, "Wednesday, November 13, 2002, my husband Dan and I drove a van to pick up young people to bring to our church on Tallahassee's southside for the Wednesday evening service. We lived in Crawfordville, a small town just south of Tallahassee.

"Dan and I left an hour early to pick up the kids, and we arrived at church before Dale and his family came in. I remember so well where we were sitting and the thoughts I had as I watched him lead his family in and go to the front pews to sit with the teens. He had his uniform on, as he had to work later that evening. He walked by us with a smile and a wink. I was so proud, and I knew his dad was, too.

"Following the opening prayer, announcements, and song, the leaders and children were all dismissed to go to their classes in the fellowship hall. Our friend, David Gantt, another Tallahassee Police Department officer, was already there.

"After the usual hour, church was dismissed, and we were back in the van headed to Crawfordville to take the children home. We were unaware that Dale had been called out to an incident on the west side of Tallahassee. We were still delivering children to their homes when we received a call from church telling us to return to Tallahassee as there had been an accident, and Dale was at the hospital.

"Whoever called didn't give details, and we comforted each other by remembering Dale's motorcycle accident and that he had wound up in the hospital with a crooked grin on his face and a skinned-up body. Of course, we were worried, but we didn't look for the worst...until we drove into the hospital's parking area. There we saw what looked like five hundred cops everywhere, on the roof, on the porches, at every turn. Then we saw our pastor walking toward us. I don't remember what he said, but we knew the truth.

"We walked into the emergency room area and went up one floor. There we saw a waiting room packed with people, family members including Dale's daughter and her mother, friends, police officers, and other community leaders. The mayor was there, as was the sheriff and police chief. We only wanted to see Dale, and we did.

"Much of the blood had been wiped away from him, but it was still in all the little crevices and corners. The front of his head protruded from the bullet that entered the back of his head as he spun from the bullets hitting his body. I'll never forget trying to hold my son as I did when he was a child. I could only hold him, love him, thank God for him, and know in my heart that he had passed from a world of troubles into a world that he looked forward to joining.

"Dale's death was devastating to the Tallahassee Police Department, to his family, to his church, and to his friends in Leon and Wakulla counties. On the night of the visitation at the funeral home, the line of people who came to pay their respects stretched out for several hours. We were blessed to know that so many people had been touched in some way by his life."

Honored Forever

The evening this all occurred, Dale left the church and called in service for work, meaning, he notified TPD via his radio that he was available for calls for service. A call had been dispatched of a possible home-invasion robbery in progress. As the supervisor, he volunteered to respond with his officers. He arrived on scene first and almost immediately was confronted by the suspect. Dale was shot multiple times, and the suspect fled the scene. Other responding officers arrived, observed the vehicle, and broadcast the vehicle description. The suspect was apprehended and taken into custody.

Mrs. Green attended the trial each day. The suspect was convicted and sentenced to life in prison without the possibility of parole.

Mrs. Green went on to talk about life after Dale's death. "Dale and his family had just built their new home next door to us. My husband was terminally ill with cancer, and Dale wanted to be close to help. But following Dale's death, his father's health deteriorated rapidly.

"Thankfully, we were able to attend Dale's daughter's wedding in January. Dale's place in the wedding was filled by his dad, which was precious to all of us.

"We were also able to attend the police memorial services in Washington, D.C. in May 2003. At that time, his dad was in a wheelchair. Our daughter and her friend knew their way around Washington and drove us from their home in Knoxville, Tennessee, to Washington, D.C.

"There we were cared for and guided by the Northeast Florida Chapter of C.O.P.S. (Concerns of Police Survivors). Their director, Charles Schinholzer, and his wife had come to our home the morning following Dale's death. He was, and still is, always there to help those who have lost family members in the line of duty, as was his son in earlier years.

"Dale's dad died in late July 2003. Joni [Dale's sister] and I attended the Law Enforcement Memorial Services in Washington again in May 2004, but we haven't tried to do so since that time. We're proud to know our son's name is inscribed on that memorial wall and also on the Florida Memorial Wall behind the Old Capitol building in Tallahassee. I wrote memorial notes concerning Dale that were placed in the Fallen Officer statue also located behind the Old Capitol building. Every year I attend all the memorial services in Tallahassee, and I'm thankful that TPD still sends flowers to the National Memorial each year in Dale's memory.

"My greatest disappointment in the past two years has been the lack of state-elected leader support for the annual state memorial services held at the Capitol Building. Several high-ranking leaders in the state of Florida have been notably absent at the ceremonies. The memorial ceremony was lacking in leadership and respect by having so few state leaders in attendance. I hope that doesn't happen again. It's tragic to see those families, whose lives have been devastated by their loss, not have the attention of the state's leaders at this solemn point in their lives. I wrote a letter to a local newspaper, but for whatever reason, it was not published."

When I asked Mrs. Green to tell me why Dale had decided to become a police officer, she responded, "In high school and while attending Florida State University, Dale's love was always music. He was the drum major during his junior and senior years in high school. He never talked about becoming a police officer. But while working at a store in Tallahassee that repaired guns, he met TPD Officer Ernest Ponce De Leon. This officer was killed in the line of duty in 1988. Dale became a police officer after this officer's death, and I can't help thinking he was called by his concern for police officers and the job they do."

She added with a smile, "Dale was the Sniper Team Leader for TPD, but I feel his greatest enjoyment was the years he was a canine officer. He loved his dog Lux, who seemed to have a personality similar to Dale's, to tease and play tricks.

"I miss Dale every day of my life, and I feel sure there are many others who will say the same thing. He really did care about others, and he truly enjoyed life, but his faith was strong, and he didn't fear death. I stay in touch with my daughter-in-law and grandchildren as much as possible and will always be proud of him and his children."

A scholarship in Dale's name was created and continues for students in the Florida State University College of Criminology and Criminal Justice. They recently dedicated a memorial to eight alumni who have been killed in the line of duty. I met Mrs. Green there, as Dale's name is on the memorial. With this memorial and the others, he will be honored forever.

Thank you, Mrs. Green, for opening your heart and sharing your thoughts, and for your son's service and sacrifice.

Deputy Chief Mac Kemp

**Henderson Funeral Home/Ambulance Service:
Two Years
Wakulla County EMS: One Year
Tallahassee Memorial Hospital EMS:
Twenty-Three Years
Leon County EMS: Fifteen Years
Active Duty: Forty-One Years of Service**

With forty-one years on the job, Mac is someone who has seen his chosen career flourish into the profession that it is today. Emergency Medical Services (EMS) workers are first responders who truly save lives and often see the everyday carnage that has become all too common for them. They offer a different and often unique perspective.

I asked Mac why he chose a career in EMS. "It seems almost like EMS chose me. I was going to the local community college and was taking a required health class. Toward the end of the semester, the instructor asked me what my goals in life were. At that time, I didn't know where I was going professionally. She told me that based on what she had seen of me, she thought I would do well in her Emergency Medical Technician (EMT) class. So, I signed up and fell in love with it. My grandfather was a physician, and my grandmother always wanted me to be a doctor too, so I figured being in EMS was close enough."

Working for a Funeral Home

Mac finished his EMT training and was looking for a job in EMS. A local funeral home in Wakulla County, Florida, offered him a job working on their ambulance, and he accepted. This was 1977, and Wakulla County was a rural county just south of Tallahassee, Florida.

Mac said, "I didn't know at the time, but when I was not on an ambulance call, I was subject to body recovery for the funeral home. We also did chores around the funeral home. I quickly discovered that the funeral business was not my calling. The good thing was that the funeral home owner let me go to paramedic school, and I worked my schedule around that."

I found Mac's start in EMS of working at a funeral home interesting and asked him to explain further. "Before there was a real EMS system, funeral homes would sometimes move patients in the hearse, or bystanders would drive patients to the hospital in cars.

"In the 1960s, a movement started to build an EMS system, and funeral homes were the first to start doing it. It seemed, in a way, to be a natural fit, but there were dual purposes and very little medical training or equipment. Things were not medically driven. It was the days of 'you call, we haul.' Few safety standards, if any, and medical protocol were virtually nonexistent.

"My boss was a larger-than-life man who would walk out to the ambulance from time to time and pull out the long spine board from the truck. He would then brag that in his thirty years of picking people up, he had never used one of these devices. I believed him. The profession has certainly changed for the better."

A New Job with EMS

While working at the funeral home, Mac was offered a job with Wakulla County EMS. The job paid more, and "I didn't have to do body recovery. It was here where I finished my paramedic training and became licensed. I was one of the first licensed paramedics in Florida. My state licensing registry number is very low, and some people don't believe me when I tell them my number.

"One day, I was on a call with Wakulla EMS where we transported a patient to the Tallahassee Memorial Hospital (TMH). After we dropped off our patient, the director of TMH EMS stopped me and asked if I would like to work for them. It was amazing. It was more than twice the pay, a great opportunity, and they were asking me. Of course, I took the job, and that really pushed my career forward.

Mac worked on an ambulance for several years as a paramedic and charge paramedic, who rides in the back with the patient. He answered every emergency call imaginable. His experience grew tremendously once he began working with TMH EMS. After a few years, he was promoted to assistant supervisor, backing up ambulances on critical calls for medical issues, such as cardiac arrests and shootings. He volunteered to become the first EMS training officer for EMS at the hospital.

Fifteen years ago, TMH announced they were closing their emergency ambulance service and that we would all be laid off depending on who took EMS over. Fortunately, Leon County decided to take it over. A position was eventually created, and I was interviewed and hired as the EMS Training and Quality Management Officer.

This was new territory for EMS. Mac explained, "I developed one of the first quality management systems for an EMS system in the nation. We did this because the hospital was inspected by the Joint Commission for the Accreditation of Hospitals (JCAH). They asked me to develop standards for EMS based on JCAH standards, and I did that. Eventually, I became third in command at TMH EMS."

Once Leon County Emergency Medical Services (LCEMS) was formed, and Mac began working for them, his responsibilities grew. He said, "I eventually moved from Quality Management Officer to deputy chief, second in command, and remain at that rank today. I've been responsible in the past for all EMS operations in the county. Today, I'm in charge of Clinical Affairs. I run the Clinical Performance Improvement Program, write all grants, develop new special projects, do research, help write protocols, follow EMS legislation, and I coordinate with state and local entities.

"Currently, I'm the Chair of the Florida EMS Advisory Council that provides advice and direction to the State of Florida Department of Health and the State of Florida Surgeon General. I'm on several state and national EMS committees and a member of the newly formed Florida Department of Health Trauma Center Advisory Council. LCEMS has one-hundred-sixty employees, thirty ambulances, fifteen support vehicles, and four response/disaster response vehicles."

Boredom to Terror

After forty years working in this profession, I asked Mac what he felt was the most difficult part of his job. "Someone has said that this job is ninety percent sheer boredom and ten percent sheer terror. Not far from the truth. Stress builds up over time.

There is a cumulative effect of continually seeing man's inhumanity to man: senseless violence, extreme poverty, and things that are just not fair. Much of this job is dealing with people when they're at their worst. They're in pain; they've had loss; and things have not gone as planned.

"I learned over time to try to minimize my exposure to the bad things. If someone was dead on a scene, and I didn't need to check them out, I began choosing not to go look. When others would go to the morgue to see the results of terrible things, I chose not to go. I segmented as much of the negatives I could control away from me. I think that has helped me survive in a job where there is so much negative stress and things that get you down. I've tried to live a balanced life. I don't even watch horror movies. I think I've seen enough horror for real."

While there are negatives, everyone can just as easily tell you the best, or most rewarding, part of their job. Mac said, "No doubt the most rewarding thing is helping people. I've been present when many people have been revived or otherwise saved from death. It's a feeling like none other. To watch someone that's clinically dead come back to life is amazing. While I have experienced this many, many times, I think there's also the routine things we take for granted that are very rewarding also.

"Just helping an elderly person back into their bed or taking the time to care about someone who's not having a medical emergency but really is lonely and depressed, are just as rewarding. I've felt extremely privileged by being there for someone's need, such as making an ambulance trip as painless as possible for a child who's scared and hurting, or maybe taking someone on the last ride they'll ever take as they're dying

As first responders during hurricanes, scheduled days off are often canceled, and extended work shifts are common. Mac said, "I have worked countless hurricanes. While everyone else is evacuating, I have always been going into work. It seems natural to me to be working while everyone else is off.

"During Hurricane Hermine, I went to work and didn't go home for a couple of days. I stayed at the office and slept under my desk on a blow-up mattress in the Emergency Operations Center. Everyone in our department did the same and was sleeping in hallways, offices, and bunk rooms. There wasn't a lot of rest, but we knew we were ready to respond to the public when needed.

"I'm not sure the public really understands how disrupted the life of a first responder can get. No matter what's occurring personally, you have to put all that aside and go to work because that's your job. Protecting and helping the public is your priority, often leaving your own family."

"I haven't deployed to other areas myself, but I have sent other LCEMS teams many times. Being in administration now, that's part of what I do. We help other areas affected by disasters whenever we can, and other agencies do the same for us."

I usually write these stories with a specific order in mind. Many people in the public sector tell me they really have no idea what certifications or training are required or what roles specific jobs play. Once I describe those aspects, I get into the more personal side of the individuals who do those jobs.

That is truly the purpose of my books, to not only educate but also to help people realize that first responders are people just like them, who do these jobs, and there is often an emotional toll.

An Eerie House Fire

When asked about his own career-defining moments, Mac mentioned two. He felt that including both was appropriate.

Mac described the first one. "I was working the third shift at TMH EMS, and my partner and I got a call to a house fire. We didn't know if anyone was hurt, but we took off with lights and siren. I was driving, and he was in the 'charge' position.

"As we pulled up to the scene, we saw that the house was fully involved, or completely engulfed in flames, and fire was shooting up into the heavens. We were in a poorer side of town, and the houses were small. This house was burning furiously, and it was very bright. We parked on the road in front of the house while keeping a couple of hundred feet from the burning house. As we got out of the truck, I saw three people standing side by side at the edge of the road, a woman with a man flanked on each side. They were facing the road, not the house.

"I can remember this clearly to this day. The three of them standing silently, but behind them the fire was raging with incredible intensity. It was very bright, and we were struck by the heat of the fire on our faces. The fire crackled loudly and consistently, but those three people wore stone looks on their faces. It was a very cold night, but the heat from the flames was very strong.

"My partner and I then noticed that the woman was holding a bundle of burned and slightly smoking blankets in her outstretched arms. She held them out to us with a look of dread on her face. No words were spoken at all. We looked in the blankets, and in the middle of it was a very small child with severe burns all over one side of its body. The blankets had burned into the skin of the child. He was attached to that bundle.

"My partner didn't say a word; he simply held out his arms and gently took the baby. I opened the door to the back of the ambulance and quickly took the straps off of the stretcher. He placed the baby in the blankets onto the stretcher and simply said, 'We need to go.' We both knew that the child, while in no real pain, was so badly burned that he wouldn't survive.

"I nodded and jumped out of the truck and took one last look at the three people still standing there. They hadn't moved. It was a surreal scene with silent parents and family and such a loud raging fire in the background. Normally, we would ask many questions, start medical procedures, and many other things, but instead, not a word was spoken. I got in the ambulance and drove to the hospital.

"That morning after ending my shift, I had a forty-five-minute drive home. When I got there, I opened the door to my house and saw my wife rocking my brand-new infant son. I instantly broke down into uncontrollable tears. Life was so unfair."

Police Officer Down

Mac's second career-defining moment involves the line-of-duty death of an officer, one of my coworkers. I have to admit that even as a law enforcement officer, I sometimes forget the far-reaching effects of certain situations.

Mac said, "The second incident caught me off guard. It was 1988; I had been through a divorce, and my father died later that year. It was a tough year.

"I was on my way to work in my personal vehicle, but I had my mobile radio on listening to calls being dispatched. I was the training officer at the time, and I had a morning meeting about different training issues. My mind was on what needed to be accomplished during my work day.

"A call went out over the radio for a police officer down. I had responded to many 'officer-down' calls in the past, but they had always been resolved by the time I had arrived. The officer may have been in a fight with a suspect or something like that, and by the time we arrived, the perpetrator was in custody, and we would check out the law enforcement officer. Sometimes they had to be transported to the hospital, but none ever had life-threatening injuries. So why should this one be any different?

"Just as the call came in, a Tallahassee Police Department squad car in front of me started to respond, very quickly, turning around and burning rubber. So, I decided to drive that way, being sure that the ambulance unit would be canceled before they arrived.

"The call didn't get canceled. Just as the first ambulance was arriving, I pulled my personal car into a large parking lot in front of a convenience store. I saw a few civilian cars in the lot and three or four police cars with the top lights on. I parked on the corner closest to the road and saw a handful of police officers with guns drawn on people lying on the ground and a couple of suspects who were partially hidden under two different cars. Some on the ground appeared to be wounded, but the cops were motioning us medics to the side of the convenience store into a small square area with very high banks all around it.

"I grabbed my gear and walked behind two police officers who had guns drawn. One was yelling loudly to my left, 'Don't move!' while the other officer to my right was yelling, 'Get out from under the car!' These demands were repeated over and over again by both officers, almost in a cadence.

"Another officer told us where to safely go, and we followed his directions to an enclosed area at the rear side of the store. We carefully walked behind these cops' backs, hoping that our presence wouldn't distract them or cause them to shoot someone, including myself. I was terrified.

The parking lot was covered in leaves several inches deep. I stepped on something that made me slip and nearly fall. I looked down and saw that it was a gun.

"I picked it up with two fingers and asked a nearby officer to take it. As I handed him the gun, I realized that none of the officers were looking at us. They were scanning the thick bushes at the top of the enclosed area. I learned that more suspects were unaccounted for. We were possible targets.

"I could then see another officer lying on the ground. His arms and legs were spread, and he was looking up to the heavens with that look I was so familiar with, the look of death. It was an officer I knew, Officer Ernie Ponce de Leon. He was a nice guy and a good cop. I had worked many scenes with him in the past. My team of medics got to work.

"I immediately started CPR on Officer Ponce de Leon, beginning with chest compressions. Blood instantly shot up into the air from the three bullet wounds in his upper left chest. While the other EMS personnel were busy with other tasks, I put one hand over all of the holes to try to stop the bleeding as I used my other hand to do the best chest compressions I could.

"I looked at the other medics, and we all knew there was no hope, but we had to try. I remember working very hard to provide the best trauma care possible, even though we realized the outcome would not be positive. It was exhausting.

"We transported him to the hospital and were met by the director of EMS and dozens and dozens of hospital personnel. From there the crowds grew, even after everyone knew Officer Ponce de Leon was dead. It was difficult to grasp. One of our own had been senselessly killed.

"I later learned that Officer Ponce de Leon had been outgunned by three individuals from up north who had broken out of prison and had picked up a fourth person along the way. The gun I had slipped on belonged to Ponce. He had drawn it but never got to fire it; he didn't have a chance.

"In the days after Officer Ponce de Leon's death, there was a stress debriefing, lots of talking with one another, and the funeral. It was one of the most grievous and difficult times I can remember. All of us medics had been feeling really bad because all of the suspects who had killed Officer Ponce de Leon had lived after we treated them, but Ponce had died. We all felt guilty about that.

"But something happened at the debriefing that really helped all of the paramedics who had been at the scene. One of the police officers told everyone that when he heard a fellow officer had been shot, he had decided he was going to shoot and kill someone when he arrived on the scene. He even went so far as to check his gun on the way to the call. But he said that when he arrived, we were already transporting Officer Ponce de Leon, and he saw all the paramedics treating the suspects.

"I looked down a long line of paramedics and saw them all tense up. Then this police officer said, 'As I watched the paramedics treating the wounds of the bad guys, that was when I realized this is what makes us different from the perpetrators. We treat them better than they treat us.'

"I then saw that entire line of paramedics relax because this officer had come to a realization that we all needed to hear. *That is what makes us different*, but such a hard lesson to learn and with such a tremendous cost.

"I remember that it rained hard at the funeral. I just thought that God was crying, too."

Honor Flight Tallahassee

Mac has spent years serving his community, one that he loves deeply. Yet away from work, he continues to give. He's heavily involved with Honor Flight Tallahassee. "I heard about this organization and began researching it because I thought it was a perfect fit for our EMS agency to help support. The program itself is very simple: for free, we fly veterans from World War II, the Korean War, and the Vietnam War to Washington D.C. to see the memorials that were built for them. That's the one and only mission.

"We started with nothing and began meeting seven years ago. We had no money and no process, but I was willing to learn. I took the idea to my boss, our chief, who liked the idea, and we made a presentation to the County Administration. They liked the idea and asked us to present it to the Leon County Commission. We did this, and the County Commission threw their support behind the organization.

"We formed a Board of Trustees of several willing and notable citizens from the community and began planning our first flight. The results have been amazing. To date, we have flown four-hundred-eighty veterans from all three wars to Washington D.C. and have raised over $750,000. We have had so many incredible experiences.

"This is such an emotional trip for these veterans since many of them have told me that they have never been thanked for their military service. These men and women, who made so many sacrifices so long ago, deserve our thanks and admiration.

"On each flight, we take eighty veterans, about seventy-two guardians to help push wheelchairs, sixty wheelchairs, oxygen tanks, cardiac monitors, medications, emergency equipment, and much more to make the trip as smooth as possible for these deserving veterans.

"We arrange for them to meet generals and other active military. A police escort is provided in Washington to get us through traffic. We feed them all meals and snacks. Most of all, we set the stage for so many complete strangers to approach these veterans and thank them for their service and sacrifice."

After a long day of visiting many different memorials, the best is saved for last. "We return to the hangar at the Tallahassee International Airport for the Hero's Welcome. Hundreds of people — friends, family, military personnel, boy scouts, girl scouts, and people who appreciate veterans, all come together to welcome these veterans home. These people wave flags, hug necks, and shake hands with these veterans. It's something you have to experience first-hand to completely appreciate.

"This has been one of the most honorable, humbling, and thrilling adventures of my life. I have made so many life-long friends. These trips give me hope that our country still has a lot of good people in it, and we still have good times ahead of us."

I asked Mac if he had any thoughts that he'd like to share with those outside of the first-responder profession. He said, "I believe that most people appreciate the work that first responders do, but they don't totally understand the commitment and sacrifice that's necessary to do these types of jobs. To give your best when everyone else is at their worst is always a challenge. To see terrible things and still go on with the job takes a special kind of courage and fortitude. It would be easy to feel that life was unfair and not worth living, but it takes a special determination to see beyond the issues of the day and look forward to a future with hope, love, and caring about your fellow human being. I feel that special bond with other first responders; they are among the best people on Earth."

Mac, thank you for your service; it is appreciated!

Division Chief Andrea Jones

Tallahassee Fire Department
Retired: Twenty-Six Years of Service

Andrea began working at the Tallahassee Fire Department (TFD) a few years after I was hired at the Tallahassee Police Department (TPD). Female police officers were still fairly new to the police department, as were female firefighters at the fire department. Andrea didn't grow up wanting to be a firefighter, and I have always found her path an interesting one. She had an amazing career and continues to give back to her community.

Education was important in Andrea's family. "It was known that if you dropped out of college, you were financially on your own. I quit school after getting my associate of arts degree in science. When I still couldn't pay my rent after working three jobs, I realized I had made a mistake.

"I got a better paying job as a bartender at a local establishment and was very happy at first. Sadly, the level of discrimination was such that I quit. I applied to a wide variety of jobs including off-shore drilling and at a mental hospital."

Andrea received a phone call from a female friend who was a firefighter at the Tallahassee Fire Department. They were hiring, and her friend thought she might like working there. Andrea said, "Basically, I applied for the job to make enough money to go back to school. But as I researched the job, I fell in love with the idea of being a firefighter before my first interview. Like most people, I thought firefighting was riding on red trucks and putting out fires.

"What I learned while doing my research was that firefighting involved strategy and tactics, and I was hooked. I still wanted to return to school, but I realized the job was more intriguing than any firefighting television show ever explored."

In 1983, Andrea was hired by the Tallahassee Fire Department as a full-time firefighter, only the third African-American female to hold that position. Like all new firefighters, Andrea had to complete basic training, which at the time was one hundred and sixty hours. It is much more now. Andrea explained, "In most of Florida, an Emergency Medical Technician certification is needed, and many departments also require paramedic certification.

"As communities recognize the fire-safety codes, and structures become safer, fewer fires and fewer large fires occur. With that, the focus of the service has changed. The amount of personnel is still required as fires are very time-sensitive, and a fast response is necessary. Therefore, the shift is that firefighters can help take on the emergency medical needs of the community."

Complexities of a Firefighter's Job

She added, "After joining TFD, I found out that the job was even more complex. The fire service has many areas. If you have an interest in fire, medical, investigations, marketing, chemistry, construction, interpersonal dynamics, the law-enforcement aspect, you name it, there is an avenue to be explored and a place for you.

"I tried to explore them all. I started as a firefighter and moved up through the ranks to retire as Division Chief of Operations. During every stage of my career, I remained connected to school. I often took classes just because it was a way to see the direction other fire departments were taking. The first class I took after being hired was a tactics class at the State of Florida Fire College in Ocala, Florida.

"On the drive to Ocala, I found out that my friend, the woman who talked to me about joining the Department, had committed suicide. This was hard to take. I had a great desire to work with this woman who had such a positive impact on my life. After completing the five-day course, I recall driving back to Tallahassee and the flood of emotions that I unknowingly suppressed came back. I cried so much that I couldn't drive. She was my mentor, and I looked up to her, and I never got the chance to show her I was worth her time or to even thank her."

As Andrea's career progressed, she was selected to serve on the Department's first Hazardous Material Team, the Honor Guard, the Crisis Debriefing Management Team, Urban Search and Rescue Team (Task Force 7), and became a Structural Technician Specialist (Task Force 7). All certified positions, such as hazardous materials, urban search and rescue, EMT/paramedic and others, require continuing education courses.

Andrea also applied for the National Fire Academy near Washington, D. C. and was accepted. The Chemistry of Hazardous Materials was the first of several two-week courses she completed.

Fire service is one of a few professions where you are allowed to sleep on the job. While law enforcement folks often joke about this with our firefighter friends, in reality, their jobs take them away from their families just as much as police officers. There are many shifts where firefighters are often awakened abruptly after only a few hours of sleep. Poor sleep over a long period of time or career can cause chronic health issues, such as increased risk of impaired cardiovascular function, obesity, diabetes, gastrointestinal problems, and a depressed immune system.

Andrea explained the work schedule at TFD. "Our shifts were twenty-four hours on duty with forty-eight hours off. There were rotating shifts that helped fill vacancies created by vacations and sick leave. Shift change was at seven p.m. Generally speaking, you miss a third of all family events and holidays."

The Fire Department's Role

When natural disasters strike, firefighters are often some of the initial first responders seen in the media. I asked Andrea to share what a fire department's responsibility is during a prevalent disaster such as a hurricane. She said, "The fire department serves a vital role in natural disasters. In response to local emergencies, we respond, assess, and act. Statewide, we are part of a team that mobilizes and is ready to respond to affected areas. We respond to disaster-declared fires outside our county, and our state-recognized specialized teams (Hazardous Material Team and FL-Urban Search and Rescue) are available to respond to other counties in Florida and Georgia.

"Hurricanes afford departments the opportunity to prepare prior to landfall. In those cases, if warranted, personal leave time for all personnel can be cancelled. Our specialized teams are required to be ready to leave with equipment and personal supplies upon short notice and must be self-sustaining for seven days.

"When a hurricane strikes an area, it's possible the emergency resources will be overwhelmed. Depending on the level of damage, outside responding fire departments are ready to fill in for the overwhelmed departments. Our department has equipment to help bridge certain gaps such as communications. We carry our own tower so that our handheld radios will work in areas away from Tallahassee."

In addition to firefighter and division chief of operations, Andrea held several other positions and ranks throughout her career: engineer, lieutenant in operations and training, battalion chief, and division chief of training. Having served in those different capacities, I asked her what the most difficult part of her job was. She said, "It's hard for me to say that any one part of the job was the hardest. I've been retired from the department for almost ten years, and what still comes to mind are the calls, the people, the situations.

"To this day, I can't pass a location where a critical incident occurred and not think about that call. There is still blood coagulating on Mission Road and an individual who burned while committing suicide on Ocala Road. The smell of radiator fluid always reminds me of blood. I remember the look on the faces of family members waiting for information on a victim. It isn't crippling, but the scenes come to mind all the time.

"The Crisis Incident Stress Management (CISM) team is a peer-driven program that allows emergency responders to talk about a stressful incident without judgement and with the assurance of confidentiality. For most of my career, I was a member of the CISM team, and I heard and envisioned many horrific calls that remain with me. I still feel for my brothers and sisters in the service who were tasked to complete unbelievable acts. I will always remember the scene that I responded to where an eight-year-old boy drowned. It badly affected a coworker, and he talked with me about the event for hours. This same coworker ended up committing suicide. It's impossible to say how much that call had to do with the taking of his own life.

"I believe that diversity has made and is making significant contributions to the fire service. It's interesting how changes that seemed enormous at the time are now matter-of-fact. I say this while I still field questions such as, "So, you were in the fire service. Did you really fight fires?" I'm pretty sure men aren't asked if they have actually fought a fire.

"The fire service, like other emergency service fields, is filled with Type-A personalities. As a triple minority, I found working in this profession complicated at times. However, I learned that good, tough, strong men aren't always tough and strong. As a supervisor, I had to provide compassion that sometimes wasn't afforded to me."

Making a Difference

I also asked Andrea what she felt was the most rewarding part of her career. She said, "With experience comes a calmness that helps a patient or victim. There have been times when I looked into someone's eyes and instantly knew I made a difference. Often, any trained person can fill in, but there were a few times in my career where I knew I was the one who should be there, and that meant a lot to me.

"The ongoing reward of the job was the teamwork. My whole life, I've felt best operating as a team. There is no better team setting than a well-organized fire or emergency scene."

Fire Prevention

Andrea and I talked about the different units in the fire department, and one in particular stood out to me: fire prevention. I found her thoughts interesting and enlightening and wanted to share them. In her words, "The beauty of fire prevention is that it speaks for those who can't. Enforcement of the codes is often a thankless job that costs businesses money, and no one likes that. Codes are based nationally on the reports written after incidents. If there is a pattern, codes are written to prevent large losses of life.

"One example is inward opening doors in public assemblies. When a fire breaks out, people can't leave because the force of the crowds prevent inward opening doors from being opened. The codes require outward opening doors for commercial structures that hold a specific number of people. In the 1980's, a large fire broke out at a hotel. It had inward opening doors, and ninety people died a few feet from safety.

"Another part of the prevention division is investigation. The majority of fire deaths occur to those who are marginalized. The poor, the elderly, and minorities tend to perish in fires more than other categories within our population. Determining the origin and cause of the fire gives a voice to those who can't speak and some amount of closure to family members."

Adversity

Every first responder has a career-defining moment, or at least a time in their career that helped shape their path. "Early in my career, I worked at a small station where I was both the only woman and the only African-American. I felt very much out of place. I worked on shift with five others I respected but heard comments such as, 'Hitler had the right idea' and that the Olympics is a communist plot.

"My supervisor at the time recently confided in me that back then, he didn't like black people. His mindset has since changed. Growing up in New Your City, I had friends whose parents had survived the Holocaust. My father barely missed the cut to compete in the same Olympics with Jesse Owens in 1936, so we watched the Olympics religiously. Statements like those were horrific to me. Though I spoke up when I heard such comments, I didn't feel like I had an avenue that would result in change.

"I wanted to leave but knew how hard the job market was for someone without a college education. It was then that I decided to stay at the Department while I returned to college. Attending school forced me to focus more on what was important at the Department, and it kept me out of the 'weeds,' or in other words, out of the drama and politics. I chose a subject I was interested in, but it was also challenging for me. As a result of my studies, the promotional testing process was easy in comparison, and promotions with opportunities to be involved in the Department in different ways followed.

"Through school, I was able to do research in Tallahassee and other locations. The team involvement in the course work and in competition was also satisfying. I was chosen to be the captain of the Seismic Design Team and we won first place for the Mid-Atlantic Region and placed second nationally.

"The adversity I experienced early in my career that led me back to school allowed me to serve as a structural technician specialist within the FL-Urban Search and Rescue program. The STS serves as an advisor to the incident commander and is tasked to point out the structural hazards of a compromised structure. Another firefighter and I were deployed to a structural collapse in Jacksonville, Florida. While taking my final college class, which was in concrete design, we had an assignment about this collapse. An article was written about it, and when I was mentioned in that article, I realized I had been brought full circle.

"Looking back, I'm grateful for the adversity I experienced. It pushed me to do things to change where I was. My supervisor at that time pressed me hard and always tested me. While his reasons are unknown to me, I still appreciate the results of his efforts. Though my comments above might cast a bad light on this crew, I consider them all to be great men and dedicated firefighters."

The Family Line

In 2009, Andrea graduated from Florida State University, the FSU-FAMU college of engineering, with a bachelor of science degree in civil engineering with a focus on structural engineering.

While working, Andrea was involved with the Children's Burn Camp. This was a camp held for child-burn victims staffed by firefighters. Now that she's retired, she serves as the chair for the board of directors for the Big Bend Homeless Coalition, as the vice-chair for the Oasis Center for Women and Girls, and as the vice-chair for the Commission on the Status on Women and Girls. As Andrea said, "I believe these non-profit organizations match my interest in helping enable others to reach their potential."

Family is important, but often even greater for first responders. Andrea said, "Family lays the foundation of support that helps you keep focus on what is important. My entire family impresses me. From creative directors of a TV network to famous and insanely talented photographers, all of my family members are my mentors. My father was a retired NYPD police officer and business owner, and my mother was a division director in social services. Both were deeply involved in the community. I grew up with knowledge of the importance of involvement. They have both passed on, but I think of them always, and it is through my actions that I keep them alive.

"My wife and I have been together for over twenty-one years. She has been my sounding board and the one who helped me see past that which is not important and allowed me to determine what is. I'm grateful that she loves the part of me that makes me a firefighter. However, she's happy for that chapter to be behind us."

I asked Andrea if she had any thoughts that she'd like to add. She said, "I feel very fortunate to have served as a firefighter. I've always felt that I had one extra component or responsibility of the job that the men didn't. I knew that I was an example to young girls who were like me when I was around their ages. They too wanted to serve as the bat boy or the school-crossing assistant but were told they couldn't because of their gender. Regardless of my rank, or how tired or busy I was, or whether or not I thought they were serious, I have and always will help others achieve their desired career as a firefighter."

Andrea, thank you for your service to your community as a firefighter and for your continued willingness to give back!

William Blanton

**Public Safety Communications Operator
Tallahassee Police Department/
Consolidated Dispatch Agency
Active Duty: Twenty-Seven Years of Service**

Dispatchers, integral parts of any first responder team, are often overlooked. Will Blanton is such a person and one of the first individuals who came to mind, for many reasons, when I was considering who should represent dispatchers in this book. I have known Will for twenty-seven years and have had the pleasure of working with him during that time. When he was hired as a dispatcher with the Tallahassee Police Department in 1991, I had already been on the job for twelve years and was assigned to the Criminal Investigation Division.

Will grew up in Ohio and enlisted in the United States Army in 1987. Trained in Nuclear, Biological, and Chemical Warfare, and Smoke Operations, he said, "I was trained to detect and decontaminate the bad stuff that kills you without an explosion and to provide smoke screening to hide the advance or retreat of troops and equipment." His main duty assignment was with the 84th Chemical Company that deployed overseas for Operation Desert Shield, which then became Desert Storm. When he returned from Desert Storm, he chose to end his active duty service and transitioned to the Florida National Guard, serving until 1994.

Will's father, Bill Blanton, was an officer with the Tallahassee Police Department. Will was raised not knowing his father and only first met him at the age of sixteen. He wanted to get to know his father better, so he moved to Tallahassee even though he still had no clear professional plans. His father suggested he consider applying for a job at the Tallahassee Police Department as a dispatcher, which offered a career path and benefits. Not knowing much about the position or what the job entailed, he applied and was selected for an interview.

After the interview, he was taken to the Communications Center for a tour. Will told me to take a moment and try to follow his visualization of this tour. He said, "My guide pressed a manual security code into the locking mechanism on the door, and then we walked in, up about four steps and into a small room. This room had low light with three rows of desks. Each desk had a standard computer monitor with a black background and green lettering. It's quite archaic to think about it now, but this was 1991, and for me that was like walking onto the deck of the Starship *Enterprise*! A large window overlooked the radio room and another looked out into the teletype room. This was an entirely new world for me."

Law Enforcement Hiring Process

The hiring process wasn't a simple one. He was applying for a serious law enforcement career that paralleled the patrol side of operations. It was an involved process that included a criminal background check and a polygraph test. According to Will, they have since added a psychological evaluation, a urinalysis, a typing test, tests that check your ability to multi-task and follow instructions, and a review of your social media accounts.

Initially, will said he was intimidated and unsure of himself. He didn't know how to type and struggled with learning technology that was new to him. Quitting wasn't an option. "Once I got my brain and my fingers to work together and function properly, it all came together." The best part was that he got to meet a whole new family, his brothers and sisters in blue.

In retrospect, Will's high school education played a role in his new career. His school had a broadcasting program that was a two-year course, and it greatly influenced his diction and radio mannerisms. More importantly, it taught him how to speak – and how to speak clearly.

From Intimidated to Training Officer

Will's career evolved, and he has been a Communications Training Officer for more than twenty years. He explained, "To become a public safety communications operator in Florida requires certification, which is two hundred thirty-two hours of training in a classroom environment. After completing the state requirements, you begin in-house, on-the-job training. Then you're rotated among the different positions with each taking seven to eight weeks. Overall, including a probation period, it takes one year before you're ready to handle all stations on your own."

Departments across the globe have different work schedules, but this is Will's: each shift is twelve hours long. He works two days, and then he's off for two days; he works three days, and then he's off for two days. This schedule is repeated, but at the end of a two-week cycle, he then gets three days off.

It's eighty-four hours every two weeks. Will said, "With staffing shortages, it's not uncommon to work five or six days without a day off resulting in excess of one hundred hours in a two-week period."

He added: "In training, we mention 'this job isn't for everyone, and everyone isn't for this job.' This isn't a euphemism; this is a fact. Most do not stay in the field of dispatch. A large percentage of people are gone by year two, and an equally large number of people leave the field by year seven with severe burnout. Long hours and mandatory overtime leaves little room for much-needed downtime. Dispatch never closes; crises and crime do not take weekends, nights, or holidays off, and neither do we. When people call 911, they expect an answer, and we are there to answer that call."

Consolidated Dispatch Agency

In 2013, Will's employment with the Tallahassee Police Department ended, technically. Our local law enforcement agencies, ambulance service, and fire department decided to streamline the dispatching process and created the Consolidated Dispatch Agency. Will was still a public safety communications operator but in a new multi-million-dollar facility with a larger group of coworkers. The Consolidated Dispatch Agency has one hundred five employees; ninety-three are dispatch/floor personnel, and twelve are administrative positions. It's quite different from when Will started in 1991.

At the Consolidated Dispatch Agency, there are five main sections: call taking, teletype, law radio, fire dispatch and medical (emergency medical services). There can be up to twenty-five people, not counting supervisors, staffing these sections on any given shift.

Will told me that each section has its own challenges and even some joys. "Call taking is stressful. Each time the phone rings, it can be anything from a stubbed toe or a lost article to someone choking, a shooting, a fire, or an explosion. There are times when you have to hold back tears as you're helping someone who has just discovered a deceased loved one. One call that has stayed with me for more than twenty years is when a parent called who had just discovered his very young daughter had hung herself. I can still hear the father's voice in my mind, in the background of the call, screaming 'she's gone.'

"You can never assume anything. Each caller deserves our undivided attention and gets it. You can be counselor, friend, confidant, or the voice of knowledge and reason. There is tragedy when someone dies no matter what you do, but there is a joy in call-taking when you help save lives, talk a suicidal caller out of committing that final act, or help little children and the elderly get the help they need. Call taking is an area where you learn to deal with people; they don't call us to say they're having a good day!"

Working the fire channels carries a different stress. Will says, "We're safe from the heat, but the tension is high when our firefighters are attacking a fire. They're talking through their masks, and you can hear their heavy breathing. When a firefighter gets injured, your heart races, but you ensure the proper support services are on their way."

Working the law enforcement channels is the most demanding. For Will, he describes it as "herding squirrels." Officers are going from call to call and crisis to crisis, but he says it's his favorite position. "I feel like a conductor in a symphony of chaos displaying, reading, and dispatching calls while other units call out on self-initiated activity and make various requests. All of this happens while keeping a calm demeanor."

Public safety communications operators also play a key role in disaster response. Living in Florida, hurricane planning and preparedness are crucial, and communications personnel are part of that plan. If Tallahassee is in the direct path of an impending storm, it is "all hands-on deck."

Will recounted how schedules were altered in 2017 for Hurricane Irma. "I had just flown in from an out-of-town trip and was supposed to be off duty the next day; however, I was contacted and had to report for work at eight p.m. that evening. I had just a few hours to secure my house and my family and then get to work. My scheduled days off were cancelled, and I was told to pack a 'go' bag to get me through at least a few days. We worked long hours for several days with people sleeping everywhere. It looked like an evacuation shelter."

People hear about police officers, firefighters, and EMS personnel working long days but give little thought to our dispatchers.

Voices Behind the Badge

Over the years, Will has advocated for public safety communications operators to be seen as part of the public safety spectrum, since many people still view their jobs as secretarial type positions. Will told me, "Dispatchers save seconds, and seconds save lives." That's a simple yet powerful statement. He added, "We as a collective group are the voices behind the badges and the lifeline between the citizens and the emergency services they need. What would happen if people called 911, and no one answered?"

For me, they are a crucial part of the first responder team. As a training officer and a supervisor, I never tolerated disrespect toward a dispatcher. That's why I've included Will in my book and consider him, and all dispatchers, part of the village of first responders.

I've asked everyone in this book to tell me what their favorite or most rewarding part of the job is. Will told me that it's difficult for him to pinpoint a specific thing, and although it may sound cliché, his favorite would truly be that he gets to help people. The following quote by Stephen Grellet was on the wall in his junior high school library, he carried it in his wallet for years and still lives by it: "I expect to pass through this world but once; any good thing therefore that I can do, or any kindness that I can show to any fellow creature, let me do it now; let me not defer or neglect it, for I shall not pass this way again." There is another French quote that is important to him that says, "What is important is invisible to the eyes."

Will said that his mother, Robin Crouch, "Was my rock growing up and is the foundation for my work ethic. Her desire to help others instilled in me the servant's heart."

From Saving Lives to Final Calls

I asked Will what he would describe as his career-defining moment. He struggled with this too, saying he wouldn't know what to pick, as there have been so many positives and highs. He mentioned talking a homicide suspect out of a motel room, talking a suicidal person out of committing that life-ending act, being asked on more than one occasion to dispatch the final call for police officers and firefighters killed in the line of duty, or perhaps being recognized as the Public Safety Dispatcher of the Year for the Big Bend of Florida. There were other instances – all equally important to him.

He described the most difficult part of his job as stress, emotionally and physically. He added these thoughts to the physical side of the job. "Sitting or standing at your desk for twelve hours a day plus overtime is hard on the body. There are long-term risks of wearing a headset, inactivity can cause obesity and heart issues, and let's not forget PTSD (Post Traumatic Stress Disorder). The human mind is not designed to handle that many crises without release. One of the reasons I continue to stay active is to fight off the ill effects of the job."

As Will stated, staying active and having other outlets is imperative for any dispatcher or first responder in staying healthy and managing their stress. He's a black belt in the karate style Upkudo, loves to cycle, and has volunteered with Habitat for Humanity. During the Christmas holidays, he often volunteers at a local charity that helps families in need. Because of his great voice, he has been asked to emcee trivia night at a local establishment, and perhaps his most unique hobby has been as a roller derby announcer for the past twelve years. He is the longest tenured roller derby announcer in the state of Florida. Roller derby is where he earned his nickname, "Showtime!"

But he added, "I could not survive this career without the support of my wife of twenty years, Michelle. She is kind and loving and knows that I may not come home talking about the nuances of my day, but those times that I do, she is there to listen and be my support and sounding board. Our pets make me laugh, and they are great stress reducers in their own ways."

Help Me Help You

I asked Will if he had any thoughts that he'd like to pass on to those outside the first responder world. He asked these two things: "If you call 911, please listen to what is being asked. Being argumentative about the questions being asked only slows down the response time of getting help to you. We want to help you, but like the quote says, 'Help me help you.' Also, please teach young children the basics, such as their name, parents' names, address of where you live, and phone numbers. These simple things can and do help us get help to you faster."

For me, William Blanton will always be family and an integral part of the village of first responders. In my opinion, he is one of those people whom others in his profession should strive to emulate. When we were in crisis mode, I loved hearing his voice on the other end of the radio. He truly was for me, and is now, that calm voice in the dark—every first responder's life line.

Thank you, Will, for your service to your country and to your community!

Andy Parker

**Tallahassee Police Department: Seven Years
Deputy Director in Charge of the
Investigations Division
Raleigh-Wake City/County Bureau of
Identification: Twenty-Two Years
Active Duty: Twenty-Nine Years of Service**

I have known Andy for several years, longer than I actually thought until I began writing his story. We met when Andy was working in the Forensic Unit at the Tallahassee Police Department, and I was a sergeant in our Criminal Investigation Division. When I moved to the Homicide Unit, we spent long hours and days working together on many cases.

Andy began his forensic career working in the mail room at the Florida Department of Law Enforcement in 1989, but left the agency as a fingerprint analyst. He was attending Florida State University, taking classes in the College of Criminology and

Criminal Justice. A requirement of his education was a semester-long internship, which he completed at the Tallahassee Police Department in our Forensic Unit. This is where Andy found his calling.

"Forensics Found Me"

He says, "I wish I could say I had this master plan all along to have a career in forensics, but that is simply not the case. Truthfully, forensics found me. When I interned at the Tallahassee Police Department, I found that I loved it and maybe had an aptitude for it. I love it as much or more today than I ever have."

While working at the Tallahassee Police Department, Andy received invaluable on-the-job training, attended training classes, and honed his skills. "Our duties and responsibilities as a member of the Forensic Unit were the preservation, documentation, and collection of items of physical evidence from crime scenes."

He rotated working on call with other members of the Forensic Unit. When on call, they worked an afternoon shift and were available to be called out to any crime scene after normal business hours. The on-call person was responsible, by themselves, for all forensic needs by the police department for the entire city. This, of course, meant being tethered to a police radio, cell phone, and pager. Responding to a crime scene at three a.m. was not uncommon when they were on call.

Some people envision a crime scene technician as someone who responds to a scene and throws magic powder around and takes pictures. That is somewhat accurate; however, there's no magic powder but instead specific techniques with special types of powder. They do in fact take photographs, but these too are quite specific, and the equipment is expensive.

His duties, as well as the others in the unit, included logging evidence into the property and evidence facility, processing evidence, attending and documenting autopsies, writing reports, and testifying in court. And that's not a complete list.

Andy earned a promotion to Forensics Specialist II, continued taking classes, and became a Latent Print Examiner and Footwear Examiner. He also developed an interest in Forensic Entomology. This led to an amazing opportunity for him.

The Body Farm

He applied for an opportunity to spend one week working at the University of Tennessee Forensic Anthropology Research Facility, commonly known as "The Body Farm." He was chosen to assist Dr. Jason Byrd and Dr. Neal Haskell who were studying entomological evidence as part of a National Institute of Justice grant. Andy said, "I spent a week collecting maggots to be categorized by Forensic Entomologists."

There are several body farms located in the United States now, but the facility at the University of Tennessee is the original. Much like medical schools, bodies are donated each year to this facility, specifically for the study of the decomposition of human remains. There are several stages of decomposition of a human body, and different conditions factor into this, including insect activity. These varying stages of decomposition often played an important part in our death investigations in the Homicide Unit. The facility at the University of Tennessee is also used to train law enforcement professionals, such as Forensic Technicians, in crime scene skills and techniques.

Latent Print and Footwear Certification

At one point, Andy was one of fewer than forty individuals in the world who were both Latent Print and Footwear certified by the International Association for Identification, a forensic professional association. He has more than one thousand hours of training in several different disciplines of forensic science, including forensic entomology, forensic anthropology, forensic ridgeology (fingerprints), crime scene reconstruction, blood stain pattern interpretation, advanced homicide investigation, shooting incident reconstruction, and footwear impression evidence, to name just a few. Andy has been recognized as an expert more than ninety times in federal court, the state of Florida, and the state of North Carolina. As I mentioned at the beginning of Andy's story, a crime scene technician or forensic specialist does so much more than "throw powder and take pictures."

Wanting to expand his career, Andy began looking for available opportunities. After seven years with the Tallahassee Police Department, he was hired in 2002 by the Raleigh-Wake County City/County Bureau of Identification located in North Carolina. He was hired specifically as a latent print and footwear examiner. In 2005, Andy was promoted to Latent Print Unit Supervisor, and in 2008 to his current position, Deputy Director.

Andy described his current position: "We are a lab with eighty-one employees. We provide crime scene processing, latent print examination, footwear examination, computer forensics, DWI blood alcohol/drug analysis, solid dose chemistry analysis, facial recognition, and ballistic analysis for the Raleigh/Wake law enforcement community. Wake County is eight hundred and sixty-four square miles, and its population is a little over one million. Our bureau has jurisdictional authority over the entire county. Specifically, I manage the crime scene agents. There are twenty-three of us in the Investigations Division."

Crime Scene Management

With Andy's position as deputy director, he is no longer on call as he was at the beginning of his career. He has twenty-two crime scene investigators who provide services to forty-three different law enforcement agencies including local, state, and federal ones. He explained their work schedule. "These agents rotate from day shift to night shift every two weeks and work eleven-and-a-half-hour to thirteen-hour days. Without going into great detail, they work two days on, two days off, work three days followed by two days off with a full weekend off every two weeks. Only a few are on call, and those people have specialized training in shooting reconstruction, entomological evidence/surface skeletal/buried bodies collection, and blood stain interpretation." It certainly is not a Monday through Friday, eight a.m. to five p.m. work schedule, and it isn't easy.

As with everyone in the book, I asked Andy what he felt was the most rewarding part of his job, and he told me, "I am an extremely blessed individual who gets to wake up every day, go to work, and do what he loves and gets paid to do it. The most rewarding part is assisting in finding the truth and representing those who can't help themselves, living or deceased."

He described the most difficult part of his job. "It's having to deal with the horrible things we see that people do to one another. Child victims are the hardest. You have to learn to compartmentalize those atrocities, and carrying on with 'normal' life can be a challenge at times. There are things that, frankly, we as humans should not have to see or be exposed to, and yet our job demands it. The sight and smell of a decomposing human being is putrid at best. I think some of us have the ability not to carry those atrocities home and let it impact our home lives negatively. My wife and children have no intimate understanding of what I did or do now, or what other first responders do. For me personally, that is a healthy boundary."

But Andy does understand the impact that this job can and does have on those who do it. He added, "I am confident that divorce and substance abuse in law enforcement and related fields such as forensics is a byproduct of dealing with these situations. I came from a world of 'suck it up' and deal with it. Thank God that old school thought process is fading away. We have a contracted psychologist who my employees can go to and speak with whenever they need to at no cost to them. We require a mandatory, once-a-year wellness check with the psychologist as well. Our mental health is so very important, and as a supervisor and leader, I feel we must provide an avenue to our employees." I'm so proud of Andy for his forward thinking on this issue.

I also ask everyone to describe what they feel is a career-defining moment for them. For Andy, it was one particular case, which I worked with him. I often use this case at speaking engagements to highlight just how important forensic people are. I was the sergeant overseeing the Homicide Unit at the Tallahassee Police Department, and Andy was a forensic specialist.

It Started with One Partial Fingerprint

We found a young woman murdered in her home. Most of the physical evidence centered around partial fingerprints, but through their diligence at the scene, one partial fingerprint led to the identification of the suspect. We worked that case for months and sadly, the investigation stalled. We had no more leads, and the investigation grew cold. Andy decided to make copies of that partial fingerprint and send it to the individual crime labs for all fifty states.

Andy told me, "I knew this suspect had to be in some agency's system. One particular crime lab had a supervisor who had his analysts create two piles of requests, one for in-state requests and one for out-of-state requests. He required them to pull out-of-state requests after so many in-state requests."

Three years later, Andy's supervisor called to tell me they had a match! The suspect was identified and was currently incarcerated in a prison in another state, serving a life sentence. The lead homicide detective, the victim advocate assigned to this case, and I had all stayed in touch with the family of our victim. To be able to provide closure and answers to this family, finally, was a gift like no other, and Andy played a huge part in that.

Andy added, "It was affirmation that hard work, dedication, and the willingness to take extra steps pays off. I will never forget the phone call I got that day from the latent print examiner at the Ohio Bureau of Criminal Investigation who provided the match. It was just one of those moments, a confirmation, that doing the right thing for the right reason, no matter how much work it is, pays dividends. We very seldom have those moments in our careers, but I will never forget it."

In a recent conversation, Andy and I marveled at how much technology has advanced in forensic science. Today, the process that Andy went through would not be necessary. With the advent of the Integrated Automated Fingerprint Identification System (IAFIS), what was once done manually can now be done electronically.

Cancer Reset My Life

For Andy, it was a personal defining moment that changed his life; it was a cancer diagnosis. He clearly remembers the day he found out. "It was June 5, 2008, my fifteenth wedding anniversary. I was diagnosed with stage-one Hodgkin's Lymphoma. I took chemotherapy treatments for six months and radiation treatments for one month. It was rough, to say the least, but as I reflect on who I am today, I can honestly say that the best thing that has ever happened to me was cancer. It was a life reset and provided a clear focus on what is and is not important: God, family, others, career, and in that order. I know now that I am living on borrowed time. As my old pastor used to say, 'All sunshine and no rain makes nothing but a desert.' Sometimes we need to face death to appreciate life in the manner that God intended it." Andy has been cancer-free for nine years!

I asked Andy if he had any thoughts he'd like to pass on to those outside the first responder world, and he provided this: "So often forensic scientists are viewed as being on the side of law enforcement or the prosecution. In truth, we are here to find just the truth, regardless of who benefits. Physical, scientific evidence does not lie."

Andy is married, and this year, he and his wife Kelly will celebrate their twenty-fifth wedding anniversary. They have two sons and one daughter. Andy's family means everything to him. He is a man of strong faith and sings in the praise and worship band at his church. As he says, "It's good for my heart and better for my soul!"

Thank you for your service, Andy; you are truly a part of the Village of First Responders!

Victim Advocate Melanie Tudor

Tallahassee Police Department
Retired: Twenty-Three Years of Service

When I chose to include victim advocates in my books, it sparked many questions as to why. In my discussions, it became clear that most really don't know what a victim advocate is or what they do.

The formal answer is this: in Florida, victim advocates provide victims of crime with emotional support, guidance, and information relating to victim's rights and available services, pursuant to and within the guidelines set forth in Florida Statute 960.

I was fortunate to have worked at a department where we had a Victim Advocate Unit. It was staffed with four full-time first responder advocates. Many departments don't have this luxury. Some utilize volunteers, and some don't have access to any advocates.

As first-responder advocates at our department, they also responded to active scenes of violent crimes, provided crisis counseling, grief counseling, made death notifications, transported victims to safe shelter, helped obtain financial assistance when needed, provided information on community resources, and acted as a liaison between law enforcement and survivors. They also assisted and supported victims during court proceedings and with obtaining domestic violence injunctions. Their interaction with victims or families can often last several years, depending on the pace of the criminal justice system.

Our Victim Advocate Unit was housed in the Criminal Investigation Division. They worked closely with all of the investigative units, the Traffic Homicide Unit, and of course the Patrol Division. The advocates were on call just like the investigators, available to handle all situations requiring their assistance after normal business hours.

When considering which advocate to represent the profession in this book, Melanie Tudor stood out as the perfect choice. Not many advocates have worked in this field for as long as she did.

Melanie knew at an early age that social work of some kind was what she wanted to do. She said, "When I was sixteen years old, I was chosen to be a part of the U.S. Census Bureau's Longitudinal Study of Women in the Work Force. I say this only because I remember what profession I told that first census worker. I told her I wanted to be a social worker, but I remember being specific about the kind of work I wanted to do. I wanted to work in the prison system, on rehabilitation, but more importantly, with the families of those incarcerated. I knew those families really needed help and guidance. I have no idea how I knew that information, but I was clear about what I wanted to do.

"As I grew up, I changed what I wanted to do and spent three years taking classes in a variety of different areas. But I always came back to some form of social work. It also changed as my life circumstances did. I married at twenty, had my first child at twenty-two, and my second at just under twenty-four.

"My husband was vice president of a corporation and the choir director of our church. I was a stay-at-home mom who, for all intents and purposes, appeared to have a great life. However, my marriage had been tumultuous, verbally and physically abusive. When I was able to reflect back and look at our history, I realized the old adage that almost everyone says—I should have seen it; I should have known.

"While we were together, I kept asking myself where I could go because I felt that no one would believe me. Then nine weeks after the birth of my second child, my then-husband left me anyway with a very sickly newborn and a just-turned two-year-old.

"I moved back in with my parents and stayed for about a year. I seriously needed all the support they had to offer. I spent the next two and a half years taking nursing classes but realized that still wasn't the path for me. I moved to Athens, Georgia, and eventually obtained my bachelor's degree in social work from the University of Georgia.

"I then moved to Tallahassee, Florida, enrolled at Florida State University, and obtained my master's degree in social work in August of 1993. I still wasn't sure how I was going to work in the field I had chosen, but I was just as sure social work was where I was supposed to be and would land.

"I discuss my past because I truly believe that we are the sum total of our life experiences, and those experiences will shape our path in life. How we act or react comes from our memory bank, and each day as we have more interactions, our memory bank increases. If you have a natural inclination in a certain area for a career, then whatever it is will seem easy for you. And that's how it has been for me in the field of social work/advocacy. But knowing how to show respect and empathy and getting into the nitty gritty, day-to-day effects of trauma and its aftermath are not what everyone should or could do."

Case Manager

Melanie's first job after graduation was with a local not-for-profit alcohol/drug inpatient/outpatient program. It was an interesting time for her, but she knew this wasn't where she wanted to be. She found a job posting by the Tallahassee Police Department for a case manager position for their Serious Habitual Offender Comprehensive Action Program (SHOCAP). Melanie applied and was hired by the Tallahassee Police Department (TPD) in 1995.

She said, "When I first started working at TPD in the position of SHOCAP case manager, the unit was assigned to the Special Operations Division. And guess who else was assigned to that division? The Victim Advocate Unit. Finally, I found 'it.'

"As I listened to stories of their cases, I was drawn more and more to them. I finally asked what I could do to help, to learn, anything. They told me that they really needed someone to help take call. So, after my six-month probationary period ended and with a lot of finagling, I was 'taking call' for the unit. I handled any situation that required the assistance of a victim advocate after five p.m. and until eight a.m." (When she didn't get any calls during those hours, she could stay home and sleep.)

Dream Job Despite a Pay Cut

"I continued working SHOCAP during the day and was part of the on-call rotation for over a year until a victim advocate position became available in the unit. I actually gave up my permanent position with SHOCAP to take a grant-funded, possible temporary position, just to do what I knew I was supposed to do. Pay cut, no benefits, no leave or sick time, and

I was the happiest I had ever been. I soaked up everything and attended every class offered at the state and national level. I obtained the Florida Attorney General's Advanced Designation for Victim Advocates. I went to classes on legal advocacy, domestic violence, homicides, human trafficking, and every other subject relevant to my profession."

Our Victim Advocate Unit had been established at TPD in 1993. It was still relatively new, and officers were still learning what this unit was about and how they fit into their jobs. Trust was an issue. Melanie and the other advocates earned the trust of the investigators and patrol officers, and the unit became an integral part of the team.

As this trust grew, so did the role of the advocates. Tasks that investigators often had to do could now be accomplished by advocates. It gave investigators additional time to focus on their own work. The advocates often became a liaison between the victims of families and the investigators. It didn't eliminate the contact; rather, it became more focused and organized.

In Florida, state law dictates which death investigations require an autopsy. Some families are adamant about not wanting an autopsy completed for various reasons, including religious ones. As an example, Melanie told this story.

"I learned a lot about culture and religions doing this job. One particular case involved the death of a young man. His parents were divorced and living on opposite sides of the country. They were of the Orthodox Judaism faith. One parent wanted their child to have an Orthodox service and for him to be buried in Israel.

"This was supposed to occur before sundown the next day. I knew this wasn't going to be possible. I reached out to someone in the department who I knew was Jewish. They put me in touch with a rabbi in town who explained all the facts to me, including "sitting shiva." I located a man who was willing to assist with the mourning process in accordance with the Jewish faith. This man sat outside of the morgue all night until the body was released.

"Certain procedures had to be followed, if possible. Fortunately, one of our associate medical examiners was well-versed in multiple religions and cultures, another godsend for me. The next step was to find a funeral director who also understood. I knew exactly who I was calling, and she didn't let me down. She was an absolute angel and treated this like it was something she did every day. The deceased couldn't be embalmed. In a short time frame, the deceased was loaded on a plane for Israel with the man who had been sitting shiva traveling with him. With all our effort, we might not have gotten him buried by sundown the day after he died, but we did it in a little over forty-eight hours. I was and am eternally grateful for all the coordinated efforts it took to complete that task."

I didn't just supervise the Homicide Unit; I also had the pleasure of supervising the Victim Advocate Unit. The above story is just one example of the type of work the advocates do. They respond to active crime scenes and often see the resulting gore just like other first responders. Melanie and I spoke of several different scenes and investigations we worked on together over the years, but there is one that for me, highlights what advocates see.

We were working a homicide scene with one deceased person. The victim's small child, a toddler, was inside the residence when it occurred. Melanie was the on-call advocate and responded to the scene. Family members had gathered, and we were placing the child with them. Melanie determined from them what items they would need for the child and where we could retrieve them from inside the residence. It was a rather bloody scene, and the victim had not yet been removed.

With the approval of our forensics team, a path was cleared for Melanie and me to retrieve what was needed for the child. I kept Melanie focused as we walked through. She too was able to see the unpleasantness. Think about this: no one ever calls a victim advocate to tell them about a good day.

Dark humor is at times a way for first responders to deal with those hideous visions. Melanie recalled, "Our dark humor was what got us through some really rough times. Outsiders wouldn't understand how we could laugh at all that we saw, but it was never about a victim or their family. It was normally about one of us, someone working on a case, and how we did something that everyone found funny. And with all of our personalities, it made for some fun times. I loved them all and all their differences. Over the years, I worked a lot of officer-involved shootings and worked with family members.

Wearing Different Hats

"As I explained to interns and new advocates, at times we wear many different hats depending on the situation. With officer-involved situations, spouses or significant others will come to the station to be near their loved one. For those incidents, it can be as simple as going to get food or just being there.

"We also worked several deaths of officers to cancer and other tragic events, the deaths of officers' children, their family members, or other department employees to terrible diseases. Not only did we help those in the community but those within our walls. The police department is no different than any other work family; we are not immune to all the negative things that life has to offer."

Melanie recalled having a particularly bad day and how a little humor helped brighten it. "I had worked a suicide the night before, and the family was arriving in town. The deceased lived in a basement apartment that he rented from a very sweet older lady. She called me to say that the parents would be there soon, and blood was on the concrete steps. I was furious as this should have been cleaned away. I didn't hold back my anger when I went to Sergeant Donna Brown.

"She told me to grab my things and took me to a store to buy a half gallon of bleach and other cleaning supplies. We then went to the location and began cleaning. We were scrubbing away when the parents arrived. While I was inside speaking with the family, Donna was outside on her hands and knees scrubbing the blood up. I couldn't look out the window because when I did, I had to stifle my laughter. It was not supposed to be Donna, but me scrubbing the blood up, but at least our efforts had the effect needed. I wasn't angry any longer, nor was I yelling."

Bonding with Families of Victims
Melanie told me there was one more case she wanted included in her story. It highlights the bond that can at times form with victims' families, especially when cases are not resolved quickly. This case was profound for me and for members of our Forensic Unit as well, but for different reasons.

A young woman was found deceased in her home. As work on-scene progressed, it was determined to be a homicide. This woman was employed in the social service arena and was a well-known, local instructor in the field. She hadn't reported to work, which was unusual, so her employer called the woman's ex-boyfriend to have him check on her. He still had a key to the home and found her deceased. Sadly, her friends were notified, and they in turn notified her parents who lived out of town. Melanie was the advocate assigned to work with the family. They had contacted the police department before we had the opportunity to notify them properly, and Melanie was playing catch up.

"As the family began arriving in town, two other advocates assisted me in meeting with the family, their friends, and especially the victim's sister. The family wanted to see the victim prior to the autopsy, not something that was allowed. The body is considered evidence, so until an autopsy was completed, it could be construed as tampering/altering evidence.

"We worked it out, and the parents decided to let their daughter's friends see her first. When they came out, they told the parents that they recommended they not go see her. Viewing a body in the morgue is not like you see on television or in the movies.

"This homicide was not solved quickly. Initially, the victim's sister and parents would come back to Tallahassee every few weeks. They had the real-life side to take care of, such as cleaning out her home so that they could sell it. I spent many a day helping them.

"After a discussion with the forensic unit, they felt it necessary to collect actual parts of the interior walls of the home and preserve them as evidence. Donna asked me to get permission from the victim's parents for this special request. The parents agreed, and holes were cut in the walls and pieces removed.

"Over time, the holes were fixed, and the house was sold. Time between the family's visits increased. But we talked often. When they did come to town, I would schedule a time for the lead investigator and Donna, and at times the forensic people, to sit down and talk about the case progression with the parents. Bonds were being formed.

"Then one afternoon, Donna called me to her office. I think I knew before I met with her. We had plenty of other cases, but I knew. A suspect was finally identified three years later. This man was serving several life sentences for other horrific crimes. We were overjoyed. All of us involved in the case crowded into

Donna's office to call the family. They knew when we called because it was Donna who made the call.

"Within forty-eight hours, two investigators were on their way to the prison our suspect was in to interview him. Now that they had his information, they were able to connect him to two other females who had also been his victims; fortunately, they had both survived. Both cases were not in Tallahassee, and before this discovery, neither had a suspect. Eventually, the suspect was brought to our jurisdiction to face sentencing. One of the best things I think we did was to bring these two other victims to Tallahassee, to be able see him and watch as he was sentenced to another life sentence, the family's choice.

"That day in court was emotional and difficult for everyone. We had to closely monitor the actions and reactions of our victim's father because he was finally face to face with the man who had killed his daughter. The family was allowed to address the court. I think most of us shed a tear. One of the other victims wanted him to face charges in her jurisdiction. The other didn't until months later because she wanted that 'closure.'

"Closure is a word I dislike. There's no closure for someone who goes through this trauma. But there is a new normal. It will never be the same as before that phone call, but it can be good again. I stayed close with these families for about two years, and then it was me who stopped communication. I can't give a good answer as to why. Perhaps I needed a 'new normal,' too."

The victim's father traveled to Tallahassee to attend my retirement ceremony. I was deeply moved and honored, and I think of it as a true, career-defining moment for me.

When I asked Melanie about the best and the worst part of her job, she said that the worst part was simply internal politics. She never understood it and why at times it could make the job that much more difficult.

Always Remember...

She was just as quick to let me know about the best part of her job and combined it with her thoughts on retiring. "I talk about these cases because it's still important for me to remember twenty-three years of meeting people on the worst day of their lives and delivering ungodly news and that I still cared. I believe I made a difference. I worked with some of the best, most caring people I have ever known. I wasn't privy to how they dealt with all the trauma we witnessed, but they showed up every day, and we did it over and over.

"I have survivors whom I've worked with for years. When they needed direction or to vent, I became a lifeline for them. I treasure them still. Some have my personal phone number, something that none of us gave out easily. For twenty-three years, one month, and nineteen days, I did what I loved, and I truly was in my element. It was the right place for me. I learned from each case I worked, not just from investigators and forensic techs, but from dispatchers who are unsung heroes. They do everything to make sure everyone on the other end of the radio is safe, but they rarely get to know 'the rest of the story.' I tried to remember that as we were ending a scene, to call or go by and talk with the dispatchers.

"To me, the other true unsung heroes are some of our funeral directors. Not all, but some of them are the finest, most caring individuals to grace this earth. They meet families shortly after we do. They have helped when we called for everything from financial assistance to balloons in the chapel.

"We're lucky in our community because the continuum of service providers makes a full circle. We're good to each other, check on each other, and most of all, try to be kind.

"I always knew I would know when it was time to retire. When Donna first approached me about telling my story for this book, I was seriously contemplating leaving. Yet when the time came to retire and I knew it was right, I had to make my retirement ceremony light and comical. This had been my life, these people were my family, and we had shared some sad times, just as in any family.

"One day I realized it was time. I had missed enough holidays and football and baseball games. I truly wanted to be present and not have to worry about the phone ringing. I don't miss those two a.m. phone calls. What I miss is the type of camaraderie you won't find anywhere else. I miss the daily interaction with my friends, my other family."

Melanie is married and has three children; the youngest is in high school. She is enjoying being an active, involved mom.

Melanie, thank you for your service to your community. Enjoy retirement, your Phase 2 of life. You've earned it.

About the Author
DONNA BROWN

Award-winning Author Donna Brown began her twenty-six-year career in law enforcement when women were still relatively new to the profession. Like most new police officers, Donna began her career working the streets, answering calls for service. She started training new recruits and turned that passion into teaching officers department-wide and community groups. When she was promoted to sergeant, she remained on the streets and continued training new recruits. Career progression moved Donna to the Criminal Investigation Division where she spent fifteen years, ten years supervising the Homicide Unit.

Donna received the Tallahassee Police Department's Award for Bravery and the Inaugural Commander and Chief's Award for Excellence, which at that time was the department's award for Officer of the Year. She was also recognized for her part of the Tallahassee Police Department's team that responded to South Florida a few days after Hurricane Andrew devastated that area.

Donna knows that there is so much more behind the badge that people don't realize or understand. She spent much of her career speaking to citizen groups in hope of educating and broadening minds about law enforcement.

She grew up in Central Florida, and moved to Tallahassee, Florida, obtaining her bachelor of science degree in criminology from Florida State University in 1979. She's a proud Seminole!

Volume I of *Behind and Beyond the Badge,* won two gold medals at the Florida Authors and Publishers President's Book Awards, a national competition, for nonfiction categories. It won two additional medals in Non-Fiction and Political/Current Events in the 2019 Florida Authors and Publishers President's Book Awards, a national book competition. Donna is a much sought-after guest speaker offering true insight on what it takes to be a first responder. She can be reached at www.behindandbeyondthebadge.com. You can also follow her on Facebook, Instagram, Twitter, and LinkedIn.

Volume II was a finalist in the International Book Awards competition for Non-fiction: True Crime. It won two additional medals in the 2019 Florida Authors and Publishers President's Book Awards.

Donna is married, and together, they enjoy spending time with their four-legged fur babies, friends, and family and playing golf.

www.ingramcontent.com/pod-product-compliance
Lightning Source LLC
Chambersburg PA
CBHW020138130526
44591CB00030B/100